Deer Drink the Moon

Deer Drink the Moon
Poems of Oregon

Liz Nakazawa
Editor

Ooligan Press
Portland

Deer Drink the Moon: Poems of Oregon
edited by Liz Nakazawa

ISBN 978-1-932010-16-9

Cover design by Abbey Gaterud.
Cover image copyright Jupiter Images / Veer.
Map design by Wayne Coffey and David Banis.
Text set in Dante MT Std and Gill Sans Std.

This publication is the product of Ooligan Press and the Publishing Program of the Center for Excellence in Writing at Portland State University. It was produced entirely by the students of this program, with mapping assistance from the Portland State University Center for Spatial Analysis and Research. For credits, see back matter.

Ooligan Press
Portland State University
P.O. Box 751
Portland, OR 97207-0751
ooligan@pdx.edu
www.publishing.pdx.edu

10 9 8 7 6 5 4 3 2 1

Printed in the United States by United Graphics Incorporated.

For Hiroki and Andre

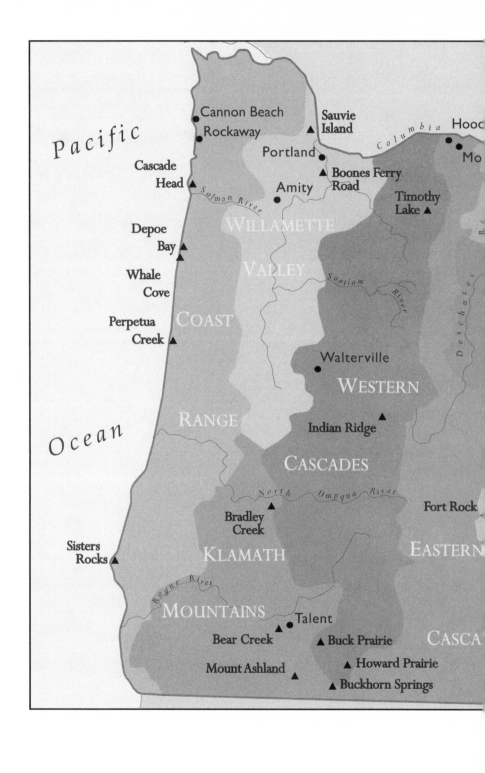

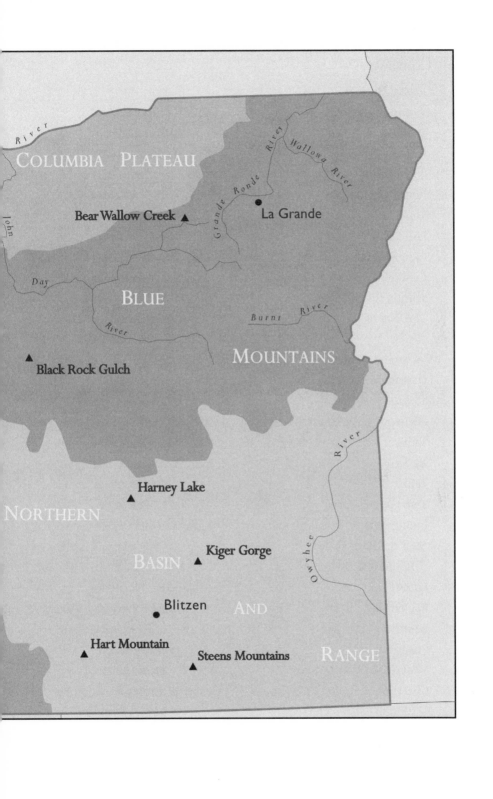

COLUMBIA PLATEAU

River

John

Bear Wallow Creek ▲

Day

BLUE

River

Black Rock Gulch ▲

MOUNTAINS

Grande Ronde

River

Wallowa River

● La Grande

Burnt River

River

NORTHERN

Harney Lake ▲

BASIN

Kiger Gorge ▲

Blitzen ●

AND

Owyhee

Hart Mountain ▲

Steens Mountains ▲

RANGE

Contents

Preface

I wanted to bring these poems together as a way to honor our state's *genius loci*, or "spirit of place," with its unique blend of geographies and climates. From the wet coastal dunes in the west to the dry creeks of the eastern border, Oregon's mosaic is generous and varied, with a myriad of landscapes and their natural inhabitants. A few special man-made places are included as well: an old barn on Boones Ferry Road, a fish factory on the coast at Astoria, and tugs on the Columbia near Hood River.

My vision for this anthology is fulfilled. The collection has breadth. Poems are inspired by places in Oregon, and each reflects the poet's relationship to a particular setting. Most poems in this collection are more timeless than contemporary and more visual than philosophical or abstract. All are enchanting.

I did not organize the book according to each poet's residence, but rather by each poem's eco-region. Poems are set in the Coastal Range, the Willamette Valley, the Cascades, the Eastern Cascade Slopes and Foothills, the Blue Mountains, the Klamath Mountains, and in the Northern Basin and Range.

The word "anthology" comes from the Greek word *anthologein* and means "a collection of flowers." I offer this book to you as a bouquet of the richest poetry celebrating Oregon, written by the poets who live here.

Acknowledgments

My deepest gratitude goes to all of the poets for their enthusiasm, help, and most of all, for their delightful poetry. The following poets have been particularly generous with their encouragement, suggestions, and faith in the project: Diane Averill, Judith Barrington, Steve Dieffenbacher, Barbara Drake, Charles Goodrich, Jim Grabill, Rick Mack, David Memmott, Eric Muller, and Kim Stafford.

Jonah Bornstein, Robert Hill Long, Barbara LaMorticella, and Dave Memmott opened the door for me to a network of remarkable poets. Early on, Ingrid Wendt encouraged me to send out the manuscript to publishers, suggested I strive for greater variety in the selection of poems, offered general advice, and provided continual moral support.

Others who helped were Ann Staley, who offered encouragement early on and assisted with the process of brainstorming a title, and Elizabeth Lyon, who explained how to write a book proposal and edited mine expertly. Thanks to Diane Averill for the title, which is taken from one of her poems.

Friends offered guidance, wisdom, and suggestions as I worked on the book: Jan Acker, Stephen Shaw, Kathleen Murrin, Rich Burklund, and Rita Conway. My sister, Mary, offered hope, enthusiasm, a gentle intelligence, and a myriad of ideas, as did my mother, Forest, and my aunt, Brenda.

I am grateful for the hard work of everyone at Ooligan Press. Celeste Thompson, head of the editing team, and Matt Walker, senior editor, assisted me through the entire publishing process with dedication, attention to detail, intelligence, perseverance, and warmth. Celeste led the editing team, helped me navigate the *Chicago Manual of Style*, was instrumental in marketing, and answered my numerous questions. Matt spent countless hours editing, designing, and refining the manuscript. He also searched for art, worked on the marketing, and organized meetings. I am deeply grateful to both of them. This is their book, too.

Coastal Range

Waiting by the Sea

William Stafford

This tidepool day you inhabit contains more than
you need. It stirs now and then to bring
faint news of old storms deeper than the earth.
From caves around you feelers and claws wave
their greeting, then slowly withdraw
    and wait for tomorrow.

Sunlight is alive when it swims down where you are,
and you stand still, alert to take in the sun.
You become a stone, then a ghost of a stone,
then the gone water's brilliant memory
    of where a stone was.

Making the day expand in your heart and return,
you play a limited part in whatever life is,
practicing for that great gift when enlightenment
comes, that long instant when the tide
    calls your name.

With Kit, Age 7, at the Beach

William Stafford

We would climb the highest dune,
from there to gaze and come down:
the ocean was performing;
we contributed our climb.

Waves leapfrogged and came
straight out of the storm.
What should our gaze mean?
Kit waited for me to decide.

Standing on such a hill,
what would you tell your child?
That was an absolute vista.
Those waves raced far, and cold.

"How far could you swim, Daddy,
in such a storm?"
"As far as was needed," I said,
and as I talked, I swam.

Walking North

Judith Barrington

for Nancy

Think of your life as a beach—
a wide, smooth-sanded Oregon beach
with the sea on your left as you walk north
and on your right a range of dunes
changing outlines from year to year.

Sometimes the sand gleams with mica;
waves slip up leaving a scalloped border
where you tread softly with bare feet.
Sometimes days come crashing in on you,
spittle from the surf flying in your face,
your boots leaving a trail of small ponds.

But always as you head for the mist-hung
headland you will reach one day—always
there's that single set of footprints ahead.
You recognize those prints: your mother made them
long ago when she walked through the years
you've come to know—thirty-five, forty-eight:
always stepping in the faint shadows of her feet.

And then they're gone. Sand stretches away
unmarked except by wind and gulls' feet:

you are as old as your mother was when she took
her final step. For a moment you wonder can you go on?
Icy wind snatches at your scarf and you stagger,
your footprints weaving among a thousand small shells.

Think of your life as a beach you can walk alone
even when mist comes down and you know you are lost.
Walking north, the cold may burn your cheeks.
But when you rest, dunes will hold you on their breasts
and two boys will be walking in the prints you left behind.

Night Beach

Peter Sears

We can all fit in one car and the dogs,
bring them. They run for the waves,
we shuffle the edges. We all
go down in darkness shivering.
I'm taking this bone wind home
for a long lean back by the fire.

Rockaway, Oregon

Leanne Grabel

Seagulls gather like an audience.
They've seen the show a thousand times
and they show it.

Meek mountains lumber
in the background
hoping for a moment
to hide behind a mist
and sleep.

Seaweed teases a billion fleas.

Mussels

Ingrid Wendt

for Ralph

We've learned where the big ones grow,
to harvest not from the tops of rocks where shells
fill with sand

to follow the tide out to the farthest reefs we can reach
and still not get wet, where last time we found
giant anemones green-sheathed and dripping under

the overhangs like the cocks of horses, we laughed, or
elephants, having each come to the same conclusion,
fresh from bed and married long enough

to say such things to each other, again
to remember the summer we first discovered mussels
big as fists protecting Sisters Rocks.

Just married and ready for anything, even
mussels were game, black as obsidian, stubbornly
clinging to rocks, to each other, their shells

so tightly together we had to force them apart
with a knife, the meat
inside a leap of orange, poppy-bright; and when

three perch in a row took the hook you'd baited
tender as liver we said we must try them ourselves
someday, if they're safe, which they weren't

all the years we lived down south: red algae in summer
tides infiltrating our chance to experiment, food without precedent,
how would we know what to do?

Counting at last on friends who had been to Europe and now
are divorced, we waded waist-deep to pick some,
scraping our knuckles raw on barnacles

none of us knowing to soak our catch two hours at least
to clean out the sand; the sand we took in with butter and lemon
cleaning our teeth for a week.

Now we can't get our fill of them.
Weekend vacations you work to the last, cooking
one more batch to freeze for fritters or stew.

Now we harvest them easily, take the right tools, wear boots
we gave to each other for birthdays so we don't have
to remember to watch out for waves

to feel barnacles unavoidably crushed underfoot
like graveyards of dentures waves have exposed, although
sometimes now I find myself

passing over the biggest, maybe because
they've already survived the reach of starfish,
blindly prowling on thousands of white-tipped canes,

or they've grown extra barnacles,
limpets, snails, baby anemones,
rock crabs hiding behind. As though

age after all counts for something
and I've grown more tender-hearted,
wanting you not to know about the cluster

I found today, for the first
time in years having taken time off from job
and housework and child care, sleeping so late

my feet got wet on the incoming tide, unexpectedly
talking aloud, saying look at that one, bigger even
than Sisters Rocks: a kind of language

marriage encourages, private as memories of mussels,
anachronistic as finding I miss you
picking mussels to take home to you

not the ones you'd pick if you could but fresh
as any young lover's bouquet and far more edible,
more than enough to last us at least a week.

Fish Factory

David Memmott

for Cindy

From dressing room with white smock
fresh from laundry, she clocks in
perfumed to smother smell of fish.
She makes a fist with clean white gloves
and joins the chorus line of slimers and butchers.
A troller glides in, bumps the dock.
Fishermen stand waist deep in heads and tails.
The jitney driver shouts down the alleyway,
look out, comin' through,
skids on wet planks
driving forks clean through the wall.
Machines belch steam as he ducks
doors of cooker blasts all morning long.
He pulls racks of melting albacore on rusted wheels
and groans through waves of heat.
At coffee, he passes down the line
sniffing ears for sweet Rose Milk.
He finds her cleaning her butcher knife
after slicing salmon into thick fillets.
She invites him home for casserole
then pirouettes, blood-plastered and wearing scales,
with the sequined flash and stun of a ballroom queen.

Cape Perpetua

Robert Hill Long

All other white noise falls beneath a private fire,
and wind in the trees, and creekwater aimed at the North
Pacific—susurrus of surf on lava as far
from me as any nebula. Where is my death,

my body's manifold declines, all my failures
to listen to loved ones, speak their names, sing for no
reason on earth? Burnt to red coals. Blown past the stars.
Perpetua Creek bears it away, all I know,

all I will never remember, to the border
where water and fire and wind first met. Consoling
to imagine how many have reached that juncture
on a late September night like this. That feeling

named by Captain Cook on Saint Perpetua's Day,
1778, as he sailed away.

Cannon Beach Meditation

Vern Rutsala

I

For years local tides measured
our lives, the sea watching
and sighing, muttering her ironic
footnotes, scattering broken
sand dollars on the beach.
We called it small change—
those shells pounded to nickels
and dimes by the surf, chickenfeed
we scorned.

II

       We kept at it though
and tonight I hold this nearly
perfect one, the last dollar
left over from those lost days.
I trace the flower it drew
on itself—almost a fleur-de-lis,
almost a snowflake. Turned around
it's the drooping leaves
of a dying plant, flipping it—
which is heads? Tails—my finger
travels tiny arroyos. They wriggle
in soft light like the lines
in our hands telling the same
senseless stories.

III

                    That lost life
stalks near me now, a life
that goes on and on like the sea.
I feel its nearness, almost smell
it in the October air—no two
leaves the same color and the sky
flying away from my reach like
everyone's lost dreams. Its long
narrow spirit never sinks and I
hear it, always walking away toward
winter, echoing.

IV

                    The shell's notched
edge ratchets me back to those days
we became tycoons, the Pacific
depositing dollar after perfect dollar
into our account. I squeeze this one,
pressing for the surf's beat,
my breathing and the sea's muttering
joined in song. Snapshots of us
catch between each breath, catch
then let go, drifting beyond memory
before another snags, lodges briefly,
then takes its turn toward oblivion.
We scoured the high tide line, dashing
into the watery ice—another one!
Another one!

V

        Our dreams came true
all week, paying us off for the years
of penny ante work we'd done culling
the dimes and pennies. I stretch
out toward those days but touch only
this shell, old and dry but still
holding a few grains of sand—like
the stubborn grains we couldn't wash off
and carried to breakfast like secret
condiments, but finally knowing we
were singled out, history's darlings
at last!

VI

        In October sleep our streets
widen and the city migrates far—
even our rooms grow, becoming parks
and playing fields, the third floor
an Everest away. Every surface stretches
thin as onion skin and lets me
hear you in your old rooms—turning
in bed, speaking your sleep language.
I almost climb the stairs to welcome
you back. But all I can do is speak
to you here and recall how we never
made such a killing again. We had
to prorate that one great haul over
all the other flat-broke summers.

And today I found only this one,
the others frittered away
by spendthrift attic shadows, I guess.
But I use this one to try to
buy back those days at cost.

VII

                       I feel
the Coast Range cringe, leaning east.
Winter sends its message along
the surface, letting the dew change
to ice on cue, putting an end
to summer's propaganda, saying I'll
be in charge soon. Then I'm paged
back to June days and the cottage
they took away in one of America's
silly games of hide and seek, taking
with it so many of our hours
of surf dreaming into our sleep,
erasing every view from those windows,
burying the calendar of those
seasons.

VIII

         Holding back winter with
one hand, I look hard for our
rich summer, moving past icy tides
and fog, digging up one and then
another, resurrecting sand castles,

letting thoughts drift out with boat
lights strung along the horizon's
dark wire. I walk all our old paths.
I fly with our AWOL kites. I want
to find each mystery footprint
and those summers locked in the closets
of the lost cottage. I grip the dollar.
I let it slow me down. I turn it
like a dial, checking each summer back
into those rooms one by one, making
them sign the register. It all seems so near now—
surf and sound, sand—and I turn the dial
one more time and we're scouring those
icy tides again—Another one! Another one!

Salmon River Estuary

Floyd Skloot

Drifting close to shore, we enter the shadow
of Cascade Head. Our kayak jitters in an eddy
as we dip and lift the double-bladed paddles
to keep ourselves steady. Lit by morning sun,
current and rising tide collide before our eyes
in swirls of foam where the river becomes
the sea. Surf seethes across a crescent of sand.
Gone now the bald eagle's scream as it leaves
a treetop aerie, the kingfisher's woody rattle,
gull's cackle, wind's hiss through mossy brush.
Light flashing through sea mist forges a shaft
of color that arcs a moment toward the horizon
and is gone. Without speaking, moving together,
we power ourselves out of the calmer dark
and stroke hard for the water's bright center
where the spring tide will carry us back upriver.

The Day of the Rainbow

Floyd Skloot

> *Until everything was rainbow, rainbow, rainbow!*
> —*Elizabeth Bishop, "The Fish"*

The day we drove straight into a rainbow
began with ocean wind and spindrift gone
wild inside Whale Cove. We saw spume glow
as though praising the memory of dawn
and waves charge the early morning air
like a storm front. Across an arc of beach
a couple walked the dark parabola where
bare trunks lay tangled beyond the tide's reach.

We saw swash drench salt-fretted sandstone
till the cliff seemed to shudder, though we knew
it was only wind stroking the grassy backbone
of Depoe Bay. Since there was a shaft of blue
sky like a quill in clouds above the headland,
and light was strong enough to hint those clouds
lacked passion for a storm, we went to stand
where the downwarped land had long ago drowned

a river that once had emptied here.
Above us two herring gulls wheeled back
and began their swoop to scavenge the shore,

heads dusky for winter, white wings tipped black,
bills agape as they rose squealing and still
hungry from the breakers. Even as the sky
absorbed them in its own granite will
we knew it was another trick of the eye—

if we held our place they would reappear
against the surf in a flash of underbelly.
But more than anything, it was the sheer
force of the gulls' appetite that made us see
the time had come to start our journey home.
From Otis to the Coast Range the Salmon River,
gorged with snowmelt, its center all foam
and silt, raised its voice as though to deliver

a curse on the new year. We guessed we were
mastering the signs since the day we drove
straight into a rainbow the rain itself never
found us. Soon we passed a hazelnut grove
near Grand Ronde and the sky before us burst
into color! The fallow valley would
have been enough to show nothing was cursed,
not when sodden wheat and onion fields could
suddenly imply a dazzle of July
in green and gold at the edge of the eye.
But we had more. We saw a rainbow span
the road. We saw that one end began
in an orchard north of Highway 99,

rising from a cluster of grape vines
like the essence of scent made visible,
and the other began in the hill

that kept our home hidden among scrub oak,
maple and Douglas fir. Despite the cloak
of clouds that blocked the sun, we saw above
us true color could hold fast as we drove,
could endure and even lead us to our door.
I thought backwards one hour to the shore
surely buried now by storm surge and tide.
I thought ahead, then put my thoughts aside.

Willamette Valley

Daybreak in Amity

Floyd Skloot

The shapes that moved outside
our door tonight were four deer
come to feed on the last winter
weeds. The riot of their flight
seemed to echo through the dark
when I left my bed to see them.

Now the valley sends its voices
up through morning mist. Cows low,
the sheep farmer's old border
collie barks as she herds strays
and the southbound freight is
an hour late. Where our hillside
plummets, a fringe of feathery
wild grasses webbed with frost
bends as though lost in prayer.

My wife built this house round
because a clear loop of moonlight
found the space for her early
on a morning like this. She woke
in her down sleeping bag under
a canopy of second growth to hear
great horned owls call from oaks
creaking in a sudden surge of wind.

When she sat up, there was a deer
standing exactly where a dowser
had told her the well should go.

Soliloquy on Rain *(a haiku series)*

Margaret Chula

Oregon spring
the tick of rain in the gutter
never stops, never stops

morning drizzle
brown caterpillars bend
the underside of weeds

days lengthen
   hoofprints of horses
fill with rain

after months of rain
the play of light and shadow
—swarm of gnats

rain-splattered fence
   a snail inches up
      to the spot of sun

Highway to the Coast

Mark Thalman

Thick and green, the hills rise
on each other's shoulders.

High ridges disappear in fog
make me wish I was born of water.

At the divide, I taste the cool ocean air,
the way a deer finds a salt lick,

and roller coaster down a narrow road
that does not believe in a straight line.

Blackberry vines
crawl through barbed wire fences.

Small towns occur like a whim.
As if in a coma, they merely survive.

I tune in the only station
and listen to country western.

Static gradually drowns the singer out.
Rounding a corner, he pops to the surface

for another breath,
simply to sink back still singing.

Fir shadows lace the road.
Bracken cascades embankments.

At the next curve, a farmhouse is half finished—
boards weathered raw. Chickens roost in a gutted Chevy.

Scattered among these hills, families
rely on small private lumber mills,

the disability or unemployment check,
the killing of an out-of-season elk.

Tanka

Margaret Chula

cascade of rocks
in the dry stone garden
louder than water
   after our fight, your fists
   clench like boulders in your lap

Tanka

Margaret Chula

this night of rain
as wind strips leaves
from their branches
I read my old poems aloud—
remember the woman I was

Tanka

Margaret Chula

after months of rain
I place a vase of red tulips
on the windowsill—
shrill cry of the peacock
ignites the darkness

Two Garden Snails

Erik Muller

On my knees, one
eye out for weeds,
one eye on them,
I garden around
a pair of snails.

How can this be
sex, what they do
so slowly, sex,
the rich cache we
mammals thrust at?
What thrills
exist in acts
this still and silent?

During a season
of creeping and
retreat, these find
a mate. I think
I read somewhere
each could enter
itself to make
babies, in case
they failed to meet.

Snails know shell life
inside out,
the high contrast
of night and noon,
shower and drought.
Nudged together,
they steadily
sip each other.

Here lie foes
of hostas, of
my hopes for leaves
perfectly shaped.
From courtesy
I let them be.

The opposite
of epitaph is
life, cool cache
of fertile eggs,
translucencies
of pinky-nail shells.
The rebegun,
ununderstood
dream comes true
in these two snails.

Immigrants

Barbara LaMorticella

A hollow of perfume in the woods so deep
I looked to see if Venus herself had come
to swim there, dropping her skirt
of strawberries and irises,

Or if some cluster of immigrant mushrooms
had sailed to the New World on the back of a log
and become so delirious with joy when they landed
they celebrated by eating their boat,
which they turned into an apricot.

After the Barn Collapsed, Boones Ferry Road

Kim Stafford

I found the swarm toiling on their comb,
slanted wall slung taut by blackberry rope
rooted to earth. It was May, honeyflow,
and the bees frantic to taste and spit,
to trample, trade mouth to mouth flowersap
their bodies held for such meeting—all women
but the drones' blunt heads bee-women fed
tongue to tongue.
               With smoke and water,
with a leaf-brush I coaxed them
into my white box. The barn would burn,
the place be scraped to raw dirt.
Only a few escaped to finger the wax
print my blade left behind, to hover
where their wall had stood and speak
their buzz twang of despair in the honey month.

Lupine

Barbara LaMorticella

Lupine—(from L. lupinus, wolf). A leguminous herb with large,
palm-like fronds. It was called "sad lupine" in the Middle Ages, because,
although its seeds are poisonous, they were eaten by the poor during times
of famine.

June lights the hills
with violet sparks:

self-heal, clover, fireweed, vetch,
and the great showy flares
of the foxglove.

But the solstice is lit by the lupine,
that lifts up its torches of ice and fire
in palms that are elegant and sad.

With its beautiful little lips
that have tasted dirt,
it whispers that the wolf of winter is moving

toward the cave where summer lies, waiting
in a skirt of sun and cherries.

Replenish

Paulann Petersen

Last night the rain held me under
a roof of sound. The night long,
rain hung its murmur over my sleep.
Dreams came and fled, each
a night-opening bloom
that shut itself back into bud
before morning arrived.

My breath and heartbeat followed
a simple-minded routine,
in, out, pull, give way.
Part of me grew
a little, more of me sank,
the lost were mostly replaced.
Rain fed whatever was mine.

Rain

Peter Sears

There is more than one rain. There is rain
that drones, how far and deep I don't know,
and rain that rattles leaves and gutters,

chattering windows. Yes, and another, wind rain,
think of wind rain, how it flattens and angles.
See, there are three rains. And what of the one

we don't hear or see, the one the brain
doesn't know—do you know this rain? Yes,
and I know another, the rain I smell

flowing the sky and I look to birds and flowers
tuning, and the air, how it slows. There are more,
listen, listen! Do you hear the deep rain?

Precision

Amy Minato

How can the violet green swallow
swoop and catch in beak the curl
of floating feather, and the beaver
chew on the ash just so
it tips and slants into the stream,
and tree frogs chirp and halt
in unison, and what makes
the shooting star's flower the same length
as the rufous hummingbird's thin beak,
and how do the eight eyes on the spider discern
on which chip of bark to press
its spinneret's wet tip, and why do
the blue-capped stamens of the pale flax huddle
so symmetrically around its pistil's cotton top,
while the sun leaves a gold egg on the altar
every solstice, and how can each tiny
winter wren repeat so elaborate
a song, and lovers fall into each other
so deft and so dumb, and especially
how can the rose campion be that exact
magenta every time.

Swallows at Walterville

Mark Thalman

Not until the sun begins to set in align
with the large willow, pump house
and back porch do they return.

Their clamor disrupting the stillness
of the plowed fields, I raise my head:
memory jolted; the song remembered
I was not aware I had forgotten.

I walk to the side of the barn,
take out my pocketknife
and carve the date into a plank
that is the calendar of their arrival
for the past twenty years.

From this time forward, each rain turns warmer.
The river courses high with a heavy runoff of snow.
I will begin planting cabbage and sweet corn tomorrow.

Cherries

Barbara LaMorticella

for William Stafford

Fireweed loves the yard
and the fire that conjured it
into the light.

And the scarlet elderberry
loves the old junkpile
        it leans against.

The morning glory smothers everything
in its embrace: the fence,
the wood workbench,
the rusted steel.

Here's a summer day that's so slow
even the light
        moves like honey:

Daisies jump fences
        and then just mill around.

Here's a cherry tree that's so rich
when it offers its heart to the birds,

every cherry
        is a year of cherries.

Letting the Sheep Out

Barbara Drake

I am letting the sheep out. They stand
behind the battered door in their August wool,
six months' growth of it, to go to pasture.
Training the dogs I tell them,
let's go put the sheep out.
The dogs run with more energy than this
small flock warrants. The sheep
would let themselves out, given a chance.

All morning they browse the pasture
turning grass into wool, lounge
in the shade of the oaks at midday
till the sky cools,
and then go back to mouthing
wild oats, the vetch drying, sixteen
kinds of grass I counted in the spring.
Sheep, you bear the weight of so much body,
like great loaves, wool most comforting,
feet small, knees knocked a little, daintily.
I never knew sheep had front teeth
on the bottom only
grinding against the tough, top plate,
wondrous machines of animal dentistry.

And their breath, like a vat of
green beer working up from those four stomachs,

a gas of eternal process.
That breath startles me with what a sheep is.

Putting them away at night
I call the dogs again, clapping to make Mollie brave
in the face of the old ewe
who can take even the young ram against the wall
of the barn like a basketball pounded
and could tackle Mollie too.

They are greedy for cracked corn and wheat
from the basins, their bedtime snack,
so they're easy.
Easy to be popular with sheep—it takes
just this pan of grain to rattle, then
watch your feet.
Toffee and Why, old matrons, ewes,
Aurora and Amity, ewe lambs,
Ajax, little black ram, ram lamb,
on account of them,
at fifty-plus, I am,
without billowing skirt,
without bonnet or curl
of porcelain or dainty crook,
incredible, a shepherdess.

Road Without Wires

Barbara Drake

Out on the road with no wires we went walking
where rose hips and apples were softening with winter
and birds flew like raindrops shook out of the treetops.
Bees that once swarmed us stayed deep in the hollows
of old oaks decaying and empty at center.
We went past the nursery where bright baby trees sat
in brave little rows, turning color as if they
knew what it all meant, getting ready for winter,
sinking their roots down, each in its small pot.
We walked past the strawberries, green still but sodden
with no hint of red from the berries long eaten
or fallen and rotten or stolen by birds who
passed over in numbers of dozens and hundreds
like minnows you see in streams in the summer
darting and flashing, then gone to the shadows.
Down the road with no wires we walked with our black dogs,
imagining time had gone backwards and we two
had rolled back with time, a wave that comes sneaking
and knocks you down gently, rolls you and takes you.
No houses, no phone poles, no pavement, just gravel
on the road between hillsides rolling and fertile.
A marsh hawk intent on finding some dinner
slid over the road with no phone poles or power wires
and shadowed our walking. The dogs looking up
was what caused us to see it. Its fierceness was fine,

a face without humor and utterly open, curious and focused
but most, I think, loving the feeling of flying.
I know that I'd like to be able to fly
but the road without wires on foot was so pleasant,
so colored by red stems and bright yellow foliage,
rose hips and red haws of hawthorn in hedges,
blue jays and woodpeckers, one red-headed sapsucker,
winter wheat sown and just coming green, black tilted hillsides,
lichen on oak trees, charcoal their branches, bare on the sky,
and with no phone wires showing, no poles and no houses,
we just kept on walking and talking like children
of memories and meals and wishes and stories,
of trips we had taken and people we knew once,
wherever thought rambled, my sweetheart and I.

The Man from the Past Visits the Present

Barbara Drake

The man who comes up the road
is tall and thin and elderly, white-haired
with glasses, doesn't look anything like
the boy he says he was when he lived here
on our farm, eighty years ago.
Fascinated, wanting to draw the missing figures
in my picture of this landscape,
I ask him about the house, the well, the trees.
He says he has never loved
any other place so well as this one
where he lived when he was two,
and which his family kept
for a retreat, till he was eighteen.
He remembers Sunday picnics,
the community of Bohemian farmers
who came together on Sundays
to play music, eat from picnic baskets.
He remembers picking almonds from these trees—
is it possible these three spindly old trees
bringing forth eight or ten nuts each year
are those? In photos he shows me I see
the familiar contour of our mountain,
much older than almond trees or any
growing thing on the place. And there
are the Bohemians, the family and friends,

men in hats and suits sitting on the hill
above where the vineyard is now, once
an orchard of peaches, plums. Their musical
instruments are cocked across their laps.
The women's dresses are long, down to their ankles.
He offers a picture of his mother
who, he tells us, stood on the rim
of the deep well his father dug by hand,
a cistern twenty feet deep to hold rainwater.
As his father filled buckets with dug dirt
his mother would pull them up from the dark hole.
We still use that cistern in the heat of summer
to water the plants in pots along the porch.

We have a lot in common, this man and I,
knowing how hard the ground is here, how dry
and ungiving except for the Oregon white oaks,
the savannah grasses, the wild rose, poison oak,
snowberries.

Dead Run

Robert Hill Long

Dogs love Pioneer Cemetery, they have the run
of its clovery, plotted mile, happy to share
with students cutting through, late for psych or dance class,
old joggers keeping one sore foot out of the grave.

No one here on leash, except the dead: theirs is grass
braided to a stony name. Old as Oregon,
a hundred fifty years of plenty rain, sun and air
enough to grow them eyes on daisy stalks, to face

this world that no longer runs from them. I don't run—
more like slow dance steps through what my body distills:
the feel of one day waltzing beyond my last will.

My dogs run this thought into the ground. The young one
racing ahead is black; the old limper is white;
their names, too, odd dance partners: *Magnolia. Midnight.*

In Praise of the Trees This Fall

James Grabill

after the death of a friend's father at 80

The yellow-gold leaves
were wild here for weeks
as if something magnificent were dying.

At the south edge of the city,
forests on each side of the freeway
were radiant, brilliant, as if the road
had meaning, wherever it was going.

And prayers that had no churches
broke out of the tigery bushes—
as if the dark days, too, will be lit,
combusting with root imperative
of words or no words and what is given
freely, without thought of return?

Some of the trees blaze in the fall
because there is nothing more to do.
There is no place other to go.
There is no other world
where we could be more whole
or wholly awake than this place
we were given our lives.

Perhaps that is some of the peace
in the body after a person dies,
that this was the world
we were waiting for, after all?

This is the world, the luminous
amber and yellow leaves say,
the edge of light turning and surging
less directly, still less directly—
until this is all there is to be?

Earth-energy burns inside all we are,
and when someone dies,
possibly after such suffering,
the peace is wild, golden,
magnificent, and then given
over to the source forever.

Born in Oregon

Mark Thalman

Some days I am a fir. Squirrels eat from my limbs.
Other days I am a rhododendron. My genes are coded
as cuneiform. Toadstools and moss grow in the caverns
of my lungs. I am accustomed to the sky,
gray as wax paper.

Tea Ceremony at the Autumn Moon

Margaret Chula

Wakai Tea School, Portland, Oregon

We gather at the tea house in the lingering
moments between seasons. The tea master
welcomes us wearing a kimono patterned
with bamboo leaves turned to orange.
In the alcove of the four-and-a-half-mat room
an arrangement of summer asters, white mums
and pampas grass. The iron kettle begins to sing.

Our trays offer a cornucopia of autumn fungi,
pearl-smooth gingko nuts, fans of rice cakes
an orange nasturtium holding the brilliance
of summer, the astringent taste of autumn.
I leave the flower untasted upon the still-
green maple leaf and, with it, a scattering
of rice kernels for the migrating geese.
In lacquerware bowls, a slice of zucchini
with sails of slivered radish—mast of fresh
chives—floats on a sea of broth.

With practiced gestures, our host wipes
the utensils, measures the tea powder,
ladles water into the bowl, and whisks
it into a froth of green. Outside the tea

house, a full moon appears and disappears
behind the clouds. I sip the bitter tea,
my reflection round and pale
in the bottom of the bowl.

Ladybugs

Charles Goodrich

Every January they re-emerge,
anchorites from within our walls,
and cloister themselves on the upstairs window
for a few weeks of fasting and travail.

By day they wander the glass
like desert mendicants, each bug
nothing but a robe and a begging bowl.

By night they huddle
in a corner of the casement,
a little heap of rosary beads,
a handful of prayers incarnate.

Winter being the season of doom,
I have my own austerities to attend to.
But, mornings, when I find
their eclipsed bodies on the windowsill,
lovely and empty as little lacquered urns,

I sweep them up with a feather duster
and return them to the garden.

Midwinter, Sauvie Island

Mark Thalman

In late afternoon, sunlight
slices between huge gray clouds
turning the valley and hills vibrant.
All colors grow equally intense
as if someone is adjusting a dial.

Each hue threatens to spill out
of the physical shape it possesses:
forest, fields, and houses
becoming a giant tide.

Across the uplands, vanes of geese
populate the air: so many
filling a piece of sky,
the eye can not count them.

Calling hungrily to each other,
they begin a large sweeping circle
for their gradual approach...

Flock after flock skims over treetops,
then descends, glides in, and just before touching down
beats wings—rowing the air—finally to settle
into wheat stubble.

Clouds heal together. Light fades.
What seems so vivid drains away.
For the first time, the geese are silent.
Some feed. Others tuck their heads beneath bent wings—
the ancestral messages of distant landmarks
surfacing and sinking in their blood.

Hop Fields in Winter

Floyd Skloot

By midsummer, twining hop vines will hide
these wires in a mob of bracts and flowers
that seem to mass in a matter of hours,
filling the dense air with a scent of pine.
But now, strung like harps, the fields sing in winds
raging downvalley. We watch as they pass
over the skin of the swollen river
and leave the impression that nothing lasts.

Brackish water ripples over the banks.
Wind tears into a stand of second growth
oak. In a moment, snow begins, thick flakes
in their smooth quadrille reminding us both
of cherry blossoms in late April let
loose in one great squall. I believe you are
thinking of spring planting as you look west
where the road bends and see the Coast Range clear.

We can feel the air warming. Where the storm
has been, morning light drenches the snowpack
before creeping toward us, nudging the dark
away. The wires wink, shiver, but hold firm.

Freezing Moon

Mark Thalman

Through a windswept field, champagne powder blows.
I walk on sculptured dunes toward the vacant road
and pause to pick up a maple seed
still attached to its wing.

There are no maples for miles.
Maybe it was dropped by a sparrow flying home.

Using the heel of my boot as a hoe,
I scrape away a crust of ice
and plant this seed under a thin layer of soil,
so that come spring
a tree might break from the ground…

rising into the air out of which it fell,
and on another night such as this
will hold the moonlight
in the snow on its branches.

Hawk, Buzzard

Erik Muller

One lifts the heart,
The other clenches
The gizzard. Both

Make gliding wide-
Winged seem easy.
Both slide shadows

As they cross
Above meadows
Between noon and you.

One picks you up
By the nape, one
Picks the bones clean.

Solstice on Multnomah Channel

Barbara LaMorticella

I thought I saw three shooting stars,
but two were only spiderwebs shining
in the rafters.

Moon at solstice, and the light
bright enough to write by!

How swiftly she travels,
pulling a dazzle of light across the water—
dabbles of light that dance, disappear
and dance...

Just as she vanishes, six white geese
paddling upstream on the river.

A Field

Diane Averill

The animal
Inside my body
Leaps over
Whatever bends in her
Path. Blue streaks
Across the sky,
A far cry
From yesterday's clouds
Where the only blue
Jaywalked my feeder.

Here, dew turns everything
Into small, multi-colored lights.
I look closely at sea-blue clover,
Find the perfect, glowing
Spiderweb. Sometimes
A trapped insect
Must break threads to continue what is
All my life.

Living Without Horses

Judith Barrington

I believe in the gift of the horse, which is magic...
—Maxine Kumin

Living without horses
is like breathing into the lungs
but never further:
never deep into the great cavity below
where horses of emerald and blue
fill the void with their squeals,
their thudding feet,
their waltzes into deep space.

To live without horses
is to slow down on the Sunset Highway
at a glimpse of chestnut rump
or a pair of pricked ears
above a bay face with a kind eye
that gazes toward the forests
draped like shawls over the Coast Range
where blue jays and woodpeckers ring out false alarms

and to breathe in the sweat and dust
of the police horse found unexpectedly
tethered to your parking meter after lunch—

then, at night, to rewind the videotape over
and over as the Budweiser commercial
sends you flying with the royal herd,
manes and tails like curtains of water,
nostrils more finely flared than the shelled human ear,

their elephantine feet
pounding the doors of a shuddering underworld
in the slowest waltz you've ever heard—
until, suddenly
you're hearing it in your abdomen
and it spills over into arteries and bones
pulsing through all your crevices
like blood from the heart's pump.

To live without horses is to carry them with you always:
the one who lifted you over the tiger trap,
the one who kicked you when you deserved it,
and the dappled gray one who lay down under you
and died as you ran away
unable to stay with him on that path
beside the golf course, breathing in
what you would search and search for in the years to come.

Three for the Blue Jays of 53rd Avenue

James Grabill

I. Blue Jay

Feathers from a blue jay some cat must have gotten
were scattered around the foot of one of the trees.
I collected them, reassembling the power a bit
in my breath, the lightness that came from the sky,
the blue that never stayed down long, the gray
and black and white that were somehow also blue.

The open sky thinks to a place on a branch,
where looking long distances lights up hazelnuts,
where quietness in the weeks can be quick enough
to live, the cleverness many feet above us,
the ancient history of this place belonging
to the birth of this blue—Blue Jay, you know
where things are hidden, and your sudden
face looks through me, back to you.
You obviously enjoy calling us outside.
Your muscular flights and landings show
one way to live with grace in a fearful world.

II. A Blue Jay Feather

In the grass behind the house, a feather glows
the scent of basil, green husks of new hazelnuts,
a steely peppermint of distant metals.

The moon flies through our neighborhood
wheeling all month with hazelnut gusts
of shape and grounding heaviness an animal feels
when he is human, the moonlight that looms
into large branches
and the cores of seeds.

Where a future breaks into flames,
it dies down into shape,
perhaps a feather, perhaps a country with squads
patrolling, the examination and operation,
the recovery time and hereafter
reaching out through lengthening day,

with what is missing encircling peripheral light
the Doug firs firmly above the molten core
of water slowly lifting into its sky of birth.

III. This Breath Reaches Us From the Future

In the back yard, blue jays land
from an unseen future. They return
for us, luminous, shaded, like athletes
on a day off. No, like strong sisters

who never bought into Social Darwinism,
or like spirit men from Peruvian heights,
breathing air full of light and darkening,
folds and unfolding, trunks and wing flashes.

As breathing arrives from the future,
fir trees hold the earth in the sky.
And some of our people go under, kayaking
down with Ernst in the undersea, pulled there

by cost or meaning, by wheels of origin sparking,
by crossings, spiraled runes, flaming root-hold
and mothering leaves, whale heads on ancient decks,
the peacock fans and nailed coins nearly invisible.

But blue jays stop easily on the ground.
The blue and shadows glow. The future
is energetic when it lands here,
and even when it is gone.

Oregon Rain

Mark Thalman

The rain trampolines on a spider's web, glistens
on the fur of a muskrat crossing the road,
bounces off the pavement like grease in a hot skillet.

The rain falls in the sleep of wheat farmers,
pulled by gravity through diaphanous spaces,
beading on umbrellas, faces cursing its name.

The rain changes to snow, white swans,
and back to rain before disappearing
into the fire.

The rain, an affliction, seeps between bones,
stiffens the joints, breaks the sun into ribbons,
becomes a word and the word evaporates on the tongue.

The rain washes volcanic dust down gutters,
drips from the cold chimney, taps methodically,
a pulse filling a bucket that must be emptied every morning.

Cascades

Up in the Mountains

Barbara Drake

Up in the mountains, rivers are little pets.
I know. I went once
along the summit trail of the Cascades
from Timothy Lake south.
Even the lakes there were small shaving mirrors,
silver spoons, icy and delicate as snowdrops.
I saw the Breitenbush River where it poured
no larger than rain from the downspout
of my own house. The Clackamas
was a ribbon of clear water I could step across.
So many rivers, and each was just a thread of silver
slipping through deep moss—
we did our balancing act, as if we, too,
were very young, on that road which was no road,
along the summit, a tightrope strung
between Clackamas meadows and the Santiam.
When we came down I was unwary.
Rivers which had been tame and small
grew full and dangerous beside me,
but I went in a dream like a maiden aunt
who remembers only the pretty infant at the christening
and doesn't recognize
the deep, indifferent giant he's become.

Age 77, I Climb to Indian Ridge's Fire Lookout Tower and Search for Lineage

Ralph Salisbury

Gestated from sand and fires
as fierce as those mating smoke
with clouds near here, glass walls,
although as clear as poets or parents alert
for danger, seem siblings of old volcanoes' stone.

Ink an eruption, of dew-drop dimension, I find
a closer kinship with the wooden tower's chronology's
sagas of growth-rings, still being written by cones
below this peak but generations of giant pines
charred to the roots, living flesh cooked to the hoofs
or claws in my brain, and any human's life
possibly only this moment, between hate
and other mistakes and love and eternity,
my family's history to date's final dot's a bee,
as black as a cindered earth, orbiting sun
in a crimson blossom, doomed
but yet a promise of centuries
of beauty for grandchildren soon to be born.

North Umpqua, Summer Run

Mark Thalman

Wading thigh-deep,
I cast a fly
which I tied last winter,
and let it drift
below the riffle.

There, a steelhead lies,
weighing the current,
balancing in one place,
the mouth slowly working
open and closed.

While eyes that have never known sleep
signal the body to rise,
slide steadily forward,
shadow flickering
over mossy stones.

In a smooth flash of motion,
deft as a blade, the fish strikes
and the surface explodes.

Trembling violently in air,
amid spray and foam,
the steelhead blazes like a mirror catching sun,

falls back, extinguishing the fire,
only to lift again,
a flame out of water.

In a long meteoric arc,
cutting a vee across the surface,
the fish, unable to dislodge the hook,
dashes instinctively downstream.

Zigzagging back and forth,
fighting the current and line,
it is only a matter of time,
until this miracle of energy
rests on its side,
gills flaring.

She's fat with roe,
so I work the barb out
and let her go
on her journey
from which
there is no escape.

Rilke Again, In the Meadow

Leanne Grabel

If I could imagine my heart as hand.
Stubby fingers balletic, not percussive.
Pads ample and open.

If I could imagine its lines
wet with trickling rivulets
teaching new cottonwood leaves how to
shimmy and glimmer.

Now I imagine a sedge's undulations
breezy and mannered.
A petting of plumage.
Butterflies, fairies presenting their grace.

If I could imagine my head like a meadow
soft, green, sweet.

Afternoon in the Canyon

George Hitchcock

The river sings in its alcoves of stone.
I cross its milky water on an old log—
Beneath me waterskaters
Dance in the mesh of roots.
Tatters of spume cling
To the bare twigs of willows.

The wind goes down.
Blue jays scream in the pines.
The drunken sun enters a dark mountainside,
Its hair full of butterflies.
Old men gutting trout
Huddle about a smoky fire.

I must fill my pockets with bright stones.

Great Tree Falling

Judith Barrington

First it totters just a bit
off balance—a little drunk
you might think, as you look
at its lacy crown against winter sky,
the smallest branches shuddering
as if they already sensed
the plunge that is about to begin
and how that plunge
will swing them in a wide arc:
sixty feet, seventy feet,
shearing off one whole side
of smaller trees on the way down.

Like a diver on a high board,
arms raised, breath gulped,
those twigs tease you,
change their minds and
hold on to the sky. The logger
sighs, yanks the cord of his chainsaw
and slips the soft blade into the notch,
cutting deeper into the heart.
Now, surely—fatally wounded
and sagging on the one leg
that has always reached for the earth's core—
now, surely, it will concede…

A crack like breaking bone,
a tremor, and the great trunk
tilts. Branches begin
to blunder through forest:
flung outward
through maple and fir,
they rip the lichen
from hemlocks, snatch at
spars, tear whole limbs from
unsuspecting spruce and hurl
the debris away into the tangle
of salmonberries and slash.

Then it slows, hangs suspended: forty-five degrees;
thirty degrees: part of heaven
soon to become earth, but for now
you hold your breath, remembering how
yesterday you tied the pink ribbon
round its hips and marked it for this moment—
how you reached around its old torso,
your cheek pressed into wet bark,
feeling for a moment that hopeless love
for what you, yourself condemned—
love, if you can call it that,
which changes nothing.

Trees Along the Highway's Edge

Paulann Petersen

From the soft-bristled fringe
        of conifer seedlings,
   to the leafy branches forming
     a tunnel of shade, they
         whip and sway
in the wake of our speed.

       Chinkapin
     mountain mahogany
   dogwood   madrone
     fir and pine
       the red-stick willow:

bless these that thrive in the
     hard wind
  of our coming and going.

Eastern Cascade Slopes and Foothills

Old-Growth Cedar

Diane Averill

Moss-covered branch with
Ancient Chinese snake-face.
Below, deer drink the moon,
Antlers a calligraphy
Of reptile talk;
One word reflects each hundred
Years of a river life.
All this, told by a bird,
Who wants us
To go from this place,
Its beak repeating a melody
That slices
Open our saw-toothed dreams.

Retrospect

Paulann Petersen

To say *dusk* is to fall short
of telling how only a coral tinge
remained on the sky, how the wind
had stilled itself to coax
meadow scent from the canal.
Our dog ran tight circles around us.
Black-crowned night herons
flushed at our approaching steps,
then returned to glide
a few feet over our heads.

We had little sense of our bodies.
Only midges tangling in our hair,
a ditchbank's uneven ground
underfoot, the air's steady
loss of heat. Lacking the power
to imagine anything's absence,
we walked. Herons startled and flew.
A killdeer rose with her familiar
ki-ree, ki-ree, and we barely
took notice—even though moment
by moment our eyes grew large,
their apertures wide enough to admit
most of the darkening world.

Provisions

Paulann Petersen

Redwing blackbirds feed
on sunflowers bent
halfway to the ground.
Hanging upside down,
they pluck and crack
dark seeds, slowly blinding
each flower's heavy eye.

I want to tell them
Wait, it's only October,
leave some seeds until
much later when
you'll need them more.

They whistle a liquid pleasure
at my niggle of caution,
my woodpile of lodgepole and fir—

they, with feathers spread
blacker than frozen stone,
with shoulders already
mantled in blood.

Falling Stars

Paulann Petersen

The thicketed stars struck up
conversations with distance,
their brief, hot scratches curved
against the sky's dome.
Zipped into a sleeping bag,
high on a bluff above the river,
I turned my face toward
this one direction of wonder.
Friction suddenly visible,
life burned itself out in streaking arcs
far above my eyes, yet I couldn't
keep from turning away.

                 Off to one side,
rising from the opposite bluff,
the huge moon: fat crescent.
Succulent cream of a moon,
big as a wide, wild
animal yawn held open
on the horizon. Risen, still rising,
and I, who'd never before wanted
to sleep in the open, chose to stay.
Outside my familiar landscape
of wallpaper, curtains, doors,
I could hear the coyotes
throw their great circle of cries

up into the air, two owls criss and cross
their voices through trees;
I could turn from moon to stars
to moon, watch them to sleep,
rouse to see them again, and go again
back to sleep in that wide outside;
then wake in morning to find
the sleeping bag, my face, hands
wet and shining with what, at dawning,
fell to the ground.

Leaf Tongues

Diane Averill

Here is the perfect green
Filbert leaf. The shadow
Of the one above it
Curves over its leaf fur.
Its body is not perfect but
The small hole in the shadow
Lets the sun drop
Its bright coin through.
Your touch turns
The surface of my skin
To lake water.
You play with my colors like sun,
Though neither of us
Is perfect here
At the end of summer.

On Fall Creek Trail

Diane Averill

A centipede moves along
The path
Ahead of me.

I slow,   watch it cross.

Each black pearl of its body
Ripples along like a necklace
On a woman's throat.

Cannery, Hood River

Janice Gould

In September, the Bartletts were trucked
from the orchards and dumped into bins
that crested with ripening fruit.

We stood for hours by our machines
as the harvest jostled by on conveyors, timed
our movements to the rhythm of the steel

peelers, feeding the cups that grabbed the pears—
six at a time—clamped them tight,
skinned, slit, and sent them to the next

group of women who sorted the halves
from the bits and quarters, trimmed the pieces
of excess hide. When the noon whistle blew,

we broke for lunch in the company cafeteria,
sat at the square tables, downed our chili,
complained about men, work, our pitiful pay
for which we were grateful, nonetheless.

On days it didn't rain, my friends and I escaped
to the grassy slope near the county library,
ate apples, dozed in the Indian Summer sun.

We could hear the tugs on the Columbia pushing
their freight of logs or grain, and sometimes
a sailboat slipped past, tacking down the river

to the Pacific. I felt the pull of a current
in my own blood, and curiosity welled in me
about what lay beyond where I could see—

but when the blast of the signal came at one,
we'd return to work, don our aprons, make haste
to our peelers at the back brick wall.

Against the din of voices, clank of cans,
and whir of machines, we stood—
guarding our unfulfilled dreams.

Dream Cycle

Janice Gould

In the dream I was asked to choose
between sky and earth, water and air.
The sky was wide and blue, warm each day,
the earth cool and dry, sweet-scented.

Between sky and earth, water and air
I could make no choice, loving them all.
The earth was cool and dry, sweet-scented.
Juniper and sage covered the hills.

I could make no choice, loving them all—
the creek ran clear like the beginning of the world,
juniper and sage covered the hills.
I wanted to breathe in every shimmering light.

The creek ran clear like the beginning of the world,
and a west wind bent the prairie grass.
I wanted to breathe in every shimmering light.
The whole world was fiercely alive—

and a west wind bent the prairie grass.
In high meadows, wild iris opened.
The whole world was fiercely alive!
Far above, an eagle was circling;

in high meadows, wild iris opened.
The sky was wide and blue, warm each day;
far above, an eagle was circling—
in the dream I was asked to choose.

Near Mosier, Oregon
Janice Gould

My bed's where the tack is stored—
saddles and hackamores,
curry combs and bits.
The good scent of horse sweat,
wool, and leather
pervade my dreams.

Nights I can't sleep,
I look out the window
at the span of heaven,
the amber light of stars
that glows in the blackest sky;

or turn the dial on the Bakelite radio,
pick up a wavering signal
from Salt Lake,
across the high plains,
or from San Francisco,
down the coast,
over the Cascade range.

I listen to a blur of voices—
barking preacher,
somber newsman,
the slick auctioneer—all
mixed with the cadence
of country swing.

But when the wind rises
and stirs the boughs
of the canyon oak
outside my window,
I tune to finer things:
rustle of leaves,
winking pulse of stars,
the shape of the wind.

Blue Mountains

Wallowa River Road, Late November

Richard Mack

the road and the river run into the canyon
where Hoffer's round barn used to stand
November is real here

black bulls and gray boulders lie
near the dead and dying
cottonwoods

heron stands where the river bends
long legs lost in the swaying reeds
and marbled swirl

coyote walks the side hill
padded feet break the frosted grass
eyes look back soft as night

pale horses and thin mist
swirl like specters
among whitewashed birches

blue jay flashes, irrevocably out of place
against juniper green
and golden willow

tamaracks die the winter death
and walk like scattered
old men on the ridge tops

mountain softens to hills
rock becomes furrowed ground
the road finds Indian Valley

soft, cold rain caresses the river
and pewter sky opens like
the ending of a dream

When the Burnt River Froze Over

David Memmott

Groundfog rising midmorning
where powder gray miners
once wheezed the dust of Lime.
I am one of them, indigent and wandering,
a frostbitten white buffalo with no memory
of the place of my birth.

Generations silently bearing up
have endured as much,
exploring boundaries to escape
the grayness of their lives.
My block feet plod through crusted snow,
stepping stones over ice, one misstep
breaking loose a floe.

Cracklines radiate; the whole mass moves.
Fissures widen and darkness seeps through.
Red willows whip fossilized cheeks,
stinging memories of shattered glass,
blood in the dreams of each small world
a hematoma, a breath

held down too long by the river's force,
dancing wobbly away under the ice.

I strip off my gray flannel shirt,
wrapped round a stone and tossed
across strong current, empty arms
loose and flapping hysterical.
It lands without body.

A resident crow scared out of a clump
of shedding cattails banks over angel hair
duskly downing white hillsides.
The black bird knows my name.
Sees behind my eyes the colors
I keep to myself:
yellow horizon of canola fields,
golden haze of sun-ripened wheat,
endless blue of wide open sky
—all absorbed into an inky winter shadow
knocking around in the trunk
of an old Plymouth body half-sunken
in the frozen Burnt River.

Awakening

George Venn

All night, while you slept, one
green tree just beyond your pane
plashes and bows and trembles

in the rain, trying not to break
in wind that never could relent.
This morning, you look out—

the wind has died, rain stopped.
One green gold life, one form,
one tree stands obvious enough.

Bold limbs begin to celebrate,
to transform light, to sweetly feed
that fine tenacious mass of roots—

fists that gripped the earth last night—
so blind, dark, invisible, below
too deep in our underworld to see.

May all the holy furious roots you
hold keep you live and green, awake
to love and give in any storm.

Boating on an Early Morning River

Richard Mack

Pre-dawn blacks and grays stole the edge from reality
    And smoke from a thousand submerged caldrons
Floated like mist among the cottonwoods
    The Grande Ronde River turned a cold shoulder
To the silent slickness as we slid into the backwater
    Watery fingers pulled us from the shore
And into the pulse of the current
    Oars cut ritualistic patterns on the surface
As aroused ducks ran away from us in unfocused splashings
    Gathering strength, the sun swept the mist into tomorrow
And turned back the blanket of today
    Lofty limbs of legless trees scratched the sky
As a muskrat slid in murky cleavage across the river
    Rounding the last corner, a great blue heron rose from the water
And became frozen in the wingbeats of memory

Connections at Bear Wallow Creek

David Memmott

Two spiders spin
over shimmering water
with limbs of soft down.

The ceremony
of Spring's vibrating wings
resolves in midair.

Spiders may not appreciate
the music they make—
only tension in lines

alerts them to light's
connections swinging
through trees.

Their tapestry tremors with dew
and windblown thistledown dismembers
their living bodies of web.

Without these thin lines
seasons do not connect,
stars drift, and the moon

falls into the sun.

Communion Before Rain

Rob Whitbeck

With gloved and sweating hands
gripped tight to the hay hooks,
we labor in the fields,
in the morning's rising heat.

And at noon,
in the shaded farmhouse,
our hands link
under the round oak table
quietly into a circle
of grace.

Pink babies, gnarly-fingered old men,
bachelors, spinsters,
lovers, widows, a common strain
of faces.

Like the windbeaten trees of the canyon
waxing on the downwind side,
we stay downwind
of time. We don't have much,
but we have a purpose.
Out under the fierce sun
there is hay to move
before rain.

Shards

Rob Whitbeck

In a haunted autumn
a great plume of dust rises
off the Palouse
where a massive crawler-drawn
tandem disk churns
the dryland earth.

In the year of our lords, '00,
power streams from seven dams
into steel and glass
city mills and plants
which glow electric in the night
and ghost the stolen soul
of the Columbia.

Above it all, on the mountain,
clouds drift, disappear
to free the down-striking light
of storm-bound stars, then drift again
to seal the sky.

Even in the world
above the trawler and plow,
above tailings and clearcuts,
there seems so little
left to touch…just heated air

rising off a gulch, or snowthaw
moving sorrow and guilt
through a coulee, the flow ending
in a catchpond, unready
for reflection.

And here and there,
along the coulee's length,
wander white and blind
assassins of avatars,
our numb feet scuffing
flakes of worked chert
and obsidian, flesh of cayuse,
now humus, and unearthed shards
of an extinguished lamp…

fragments of a Paiute skull
float out of the erosion
into the full sun,
into the full pain
that glares on so much
dimming godlight.

Genesis

Rob Whitbeck

Shrouded dawn.
Seeds swell
in a fallow stubble field.
The river slips by.
Calm at first light.
Doe wades, hooves
clatter flat wet stones.
Fawn springs in belly.
Steelhead run to spawn.
Geese lie still
in nests,
in brown reeds,
in fog.

Unspeakable—
genesis blesses
those primates, the earth's
troubled children.

The Homeland

Rob Whitbeck

Few come into these ridges
where late morning heaves up
the brutal sun of afternoon.
Grasses, cheat and medusa,
were dead before June.
Blackrock gulch, crumbling sidehill
of brown basalt, lie stained white
with alkali and lichen.
Heat waves across the draw
ripple off brittle rims,
and scattered patches of dappled shade
darken the bases
of stunted juniper
and ancient ironwood.

Few come
where diamondback eyes
search the washed light.
A tail rattles on ravine rock;
a body slithers over dust
where sun-bleached bone breaks down
into powder. Then a voice,
nearly human; a raven squalls
to lay her mark on the dead
silence…coyote listens,

ears cocked in a cool
earthen lair. A lone
northern harrier
circles and rides
the fevered, uprising air.

What appears near
is so far away.
I came alone, and stay that way.
Few see reason to be here.

Place of the Bear

Amy Minato

Just within a narrow canyon
a ponderosa glows salmon in the dusk
wide as a throne, wet piles
of berried dung strewn
like offerings around the base.

We look up the bark
to where needles and branches merge
with cloud and sky searching
for small eyes in dark hulks
of fur but find only
claw scars and a paw mark
etched at eye level onto the trunk.

Shrubs crowd the slim path
between river and rock wall where we imagine
intruding on the cornered presence
of bear near its home. A hawk screams,
a snake crosses before us, crickets
start up their dull hum and suddenly
the place seems well and long
inhabited without us.

Later, humbled by fear
but warm with soup, we lie

like temple keepers near the canyon entrance
and dizzy from bat-watching trace
the sharp points of *Ursa Major*
across the late summer sky.

Inheritance at Wheatland

Kim Stafford

A man goes over a barbwire fence,
a child under, and a woman through.
      —East Oregon saying

The yard was fenced to keep horses out,
the barbwire woven with wild rose, but her house
was built without a lock on the door—
an old custom from another time.
With a wave of her hand she gave it all
to the people in town at the end.
They came from Athena for the auction,
from Helix, Ione, La Grande—no one
old enough to know her well.
And when the horses, dressed in leather
and brass, were led away, the obsolete
thresher sold, and all the minor glories
of accumulation in an old family,
childless and done, dispersed, they
had to decide about that house,
the oldest in town, magnificent
in its desolation.

It was unsafe, leaning toward the street
from its blooming grove of locust trees.
There was talk of making it a museum.

"But you can't rebuild the past,"
said the watermelon merchants
to the City Council, and they
were right: "Preserve what's sound."
So the Fire Department volunteered
to burn it down—a practice run
to train the crew the essentials
of rescue. They'd found a doll
in the attic, wrapped in gingham,
a rude wooden face and hornbeam eyes,
and set her in the round window
niched in the west gable.
Sunday at dawn, without
warning the bell began clanging
and smoke poured from the derelict
cellar, and they all, dressing as they ran
down Main, clustered at the station
to clamber onto the truck howling
up the hill, the long automatic ladder
already lifting as it entered the yard,
the chief with an ax swaying up through smoke
toward that doll hand beckoning behind glass.
But then the roof, tinder dry and shimmering,
blossomed wide; the trees blazed up
in crowns of fire, and the round window
shattered open on a small form dressed in flames.
They pulled the ladder clear, the chief
bundled safe in asbestos boot and glove,
helmet medallion tarnished by the heat
and eyelashes singed away.

But the children arrived in time
to see that face at the eave, that hand
reach out through a veil of sparks
extending a gift of flame
when the house crumbled into itself
within the rows of burning trees.

Sparrows

George Venn

I want to tell you how the white-crown sparrows came
again. It was Earth Day morning, April 21, 2001.
After breakfast, my hands wrapped around the heat of
half-empty coffee, I sat still in my robe, stared south out

the window. From far away, the radio played Haydn
and his quartet filled the empty room with simple dignity—
no pretense, no grief—notes of quiet inspiration flowed.
Spring sun poured easy everywhere, touched all the empty

angles of Japanese quince out there in the yard. Leafless,
still, the night frost cold, the brown bark gleamed and shadowed
beyond me—just tight buds—no pink, no blossoms, no half
burst greening leaves. Just shape, form, emptiness ready to

open, to flower, give pollen, receive the bees again.
Then, sudden as some surprise doorbell ring, gray wings—
where did they come from?—came flit flit flit out of nowhere
I could see, perched there in those bare quince limbs,

wrapped their wings around themselves, wrapped their tiny
toes around those budding limbs, and sat and stared in at me,
I thought, stared from underneath the dazzle of their crowns
where black and white are one. I could not move. I gave back

their gaze as best I could. Six of them, yes, six waited there.
Were they three pairs come back to nest again? A family all
together at the end of long migratory flight? Would they live
here with me? They seemed to know the branches of the quince

they seemed to sit with some sense of home, alert, at peace,
their gray feathers fluffed, their black eyes shining. How long
we stared this way I do not know. Time disappeared from me
and I became that quince in spring, became those wild sudden

unknown lives—mine to see, receive, and never understand.

Reluctance

David Axelrod

To imagine why this man feels summoned to this field
you must dismiss the idea that the shape of any moment is random.
Rather it's an expression of intention,
what, perhaps, the universe itself desires at this time,
in this place, for this man, who not an hour ago
spoke over the phone to a nurse two thousand miles away,
her voice so clear, they may have been standing
side by side in the corridor of the hospital,
when she told him, "Your aunt is gone."

How else will I make any sense of this flock of juncos
that darts across the pasture field, a flock that seems
to have elaborated the laws of the physics of flight.
They bob in the air as if air were substantial as water
and they as light and buoyant and fragile as glass
floats riding toward me in the invisible surf—
how else will I explain feeling summoned here,
this late February, almost-spring dawn,
the dull sky spitting kernels of sleet?

Are they my guides? Am I theirs? Or does a third force
direct us all along this dirt road
from the foothills to the edge of town,
where sheltering thickets of hawthorn and roses are wild
with tart, desiccated, nut-tough fruit?

How else is it possible to explain why
one bird falls away from the flock and doesn't flee,
but splays open on the frozen road,
as though giving permission to pick her up?

And if you know that my aunt died
from an injured leg that never healed,
then what will explain—coincidence?—
this bird's twisted, withered leg, dragging beneath her?
Nothing I believe in quite prepares me for the possibility
that I hold the glass sphere of my aunt's being in my hands,
or that a benevolence at the root of matter animates events,
thus defying all the other evidence to the contrary,
my tenderness toward this bird.

Tekmerion

David Axelrod

Remind me, someone, it's only a matter of luck
whether famine inhabits a land or not,
and infallible signs in no way prepare us for a rapture
that ruptures the small world.

If I go outside at dark to dump a bowl of Empire skins in compost
and a blue halo of ice circles the Hunter Moon,
how certain may I be that flocks of geese will form by noon
the next day, a cold rain arrive by dusk?

Bent over scythe and shears, on my knees by first light,
I cut stalks of annuals, shake out seeds,
fold perennials in protest of the coming freeze
that will outlast the night.

Let fools talk loudest who hunger for wildness,
I refuse, in October, to concede,
to unhouse my mind, and choose
to hammer larch billets a little tighter in the wood pile.

A few geese squawk above the garden,
gather into one flock, turn a last circle over the valley
and dive past Glass Hill, the customary V receding,
growing small in the south, a dark filament in a sooty sky.

Unhoused at last am I, spellbound by signs
or just the usual melancholy
of knowing we'll die before we die?
Or maybe just stubborn?

Domestic provisions don't summon much confidence,
nor does chopping away last summer's dry exuberances—
I make my prayers for the small world
to endure just one more night.

And kneeling in shelter of brittle leaves
at noon, I pick and greedily eat a few raspberries
tricked into late blossom and ripening,
even as canes rattle like death's hollow bones.

I practice my lost faith because, as I pack away my tools,
a frog peeps from its cranny in the rock wall,
and all evening and all the next day,
a mellow rain trickles in gutters—

rain coming almost too late this year,
we feared it might not arrive,
the reservoir remain a mudflat valley of stumps,
the river a bed of algae-draped stones.

After the end of the end, if rains seem less random,
I can't imagine myself in this garden,
a man, who, no smarter nor dumber than the rest,
and neither guilty nor guiltless,

sees rocket, kale, and rainbow chard
unfold from rotten straw in March,
and fails to recognize these signs,
fails to feel unaccountably kind.

High Centered

Ellen Waterston

I was on my long way to somewhere
when halfway between the Equator
and the North Pole a phantasm
appeared on the low-heeled horizon
of an empty stretch of desert road.

The sign said: Welcome! Ghost town, curios, gas, ice.

I pulled over to check my progress,
idled in neutral on the roadside, dead-
centered between cold and hot. I tell
myself: just a short break in the drive.

How fast and silently time derails here.
How fast I forget to risk, feel. Along this,

the only street, tattered screens
whistle and mew in the imagined breeze.
Catawampus doors titter on a single hinge,
pretending the same thing: wind. Porch planks
yawp and yearn toward the supposed
sun. "Welcome," says the apparition and changes
the sign to read: Population: one
more.

Klamath Mountains

Winter in the Shadow of the Siskiyous, Talent

Steve Dieffenbacher

It is hours past
the gray and white
morning's rise over stiff
starlings on voiceless wires,

the day a shroud
of dull silver behind blinds
blocking the language
of ascension.

All I can hope for
is sound, the bands
of late-afternoon mustard
resolving to jabbers,

evening's undernotes
after a month's rain
when all my hunger is for violet
over the mountains

and all I can summon
are the lost swallows of summer,
the uncertain hum in the air
of imagined sunsets

while sharp squares
of light rake the floor
here under the window
with a clarity I cannot direct

or resist, a forgotten
spectrum of blind luminance
equally shadowless,
just as indifferent.

Southern Oregon, New Year's Afternoon

Vincent Wixon

The wind bites at the ranch on Windemar Drive
as trucks on I-5 ratchet up the grade to Siskiyou Summit.
Beyond the freeway snowy foothills gleam,
and Pilot Butte still witnesses the Applegate Trail.

Vacation help, I've come to feed the livestock—
one horse and two dogs—grateful to be domestic,
not pushing through that pass with tire chains
in the trunk, one of those items
whose virtue is disuse.

Like me, the animals want to be in at night.
Dottie and Goldie bark with joy,
sniff the treat in my pocket,
and the lonely horse nickers,
kicks up her heels, and heads for the barn.

On a Winter Hillside

Jonah Bornstein

Where were you when light dipped below,
Your bells ringing only when the coffins came?

Ice brightens the yellows of the field
along Bradley Creek. Walk
onto the cattle path, the swollen earth
folding into your footprints as you pass.
Climb up the hillside into the grove of stone,
where alder bark curls in sheaths of pain.
Look up the hill toward the sun, apprehend
what labors under the grass, pressing
rocks up from below.

Follow the trail to the snowline
where the ceanothus grows. Find the rusted
wire gate, horses from the other side stammering,
their tough bellies heaving against the barbs, blood
swirling like oil in the puddles beneath.

Do not turn back to what is known.
Follow the tracks into the snow,
to an ancient fire that gleams
between two stones—talismans
of lives not freely given, falling
and lifting before you on creases
of memory you've secured to dream.

Wait by the stones for the sun to set, winter to come,
to know what floats around this thinness close to your lives—

If you listen closely, as the sun crosses the crest
and light darkens in your eyes, you can hear
us sing, "Unearth our bodies. Bring your shovels,
your ropes, and burlap bags to bind our remains. Pull us home."

Hear our calling. Close your eyes.
The cold will strike.
Our empty bones will chime.

Winter Solstice, 2001

Vincent Wixon

Outside our window the wind blows.
The trumpet vine's dry pods click on the siding.

A junco bangs the window leaving a halo of down,
staggers, then takes off, flicking its white tail feathers.

The neighbor hammers upstairs flooring in his remodel
as an insulation truck grinds onto his front yard.

A hundred feet above our house, snow covers the foothills.
Tonight we'll see the ski lights ascending Mt. Ashland.

The forest has invaded the house—tree with gilded bulbs,
branches covering mantle and lining banisters.

I sit at the kitchen table, drink black tea,
open my book. I won't answer the door.

Lost on the Mountain

Patricia Wixon

In this photo of you on the mountain
where streaks of light on the gray-blue snow
blend earth and sky, it's clear you're confident

reading the topo draped over your hands,
one glove removed so you can point to the trail
above Buck Prairie. The tips of your skis

push into a drift, poles stand upright, ready.
No foreshadowing here of that other time,
except for the presence of snow, a trail, you.

We'd sat at our table watching dark
drop pines and madrone into crevasses—
deep black envelopes between the hills.

Thick snow flickered the porch light,
and our fears began: you in a whiteout.
Night looks flat without a moon.

We pulled on boots and jackets, began the drive up.
Snow banked car windows, blotting out edges.
Tires skated uselessly. We parked and walked,

arched our flashlights over the trail to swing
past trees blurred black in swirling white.
We listened hard, heard only our own steps crunch.

Would you remember to reach for uphill banks?
Or if you fell, force yourself to get up, not rest?
Our flashlights searched for tracks in a circle

like an old Western movie, back to the start.
Finally, our light found you—panic in your eyes,
sweat dripping from your nose freezing to your chin.

Each time I pass this picture, I see your eagerness.
No hint of what our memories hold: relief and solace
that stopped our words. Silence spoke enough.

Deer at 3 A.M.
Patricia Wixon

Her wild smell moves
through the screen
and wakes me before
I hear her nosing
the new escallonia.
She lifts her head,
holds it rigid,
ears like mirrors
catching the moonlight.
Did she hear me move
in bed or breathe?
We each listen
for the next signal.

The Art of Waking

Jonah Bornstein

Meditation at Howard Prairie

To rise from sleep,
the days molting from within, to stretch
toward pines circling the lake, with one breath
held beneath reflected spruce, until
there is no ascension from water. Imagine
an exit threaded to the periphery, where cattle turn
to drink from the well of their imprints.
To walk among the desolate and the ash
of last year's pelicans, the throb of wings
a memory, where dragonflies whir
locked in heat until they drop, listless
as the pulse of embers. If I could unravel
the brief excess of their mating,
I might step from the circuitry
of sleep, no longer adhering
to disfigured words, the chalky
kiss of love, our binding of earnestness.
Here, no words, no disgrace, as if today
folded back without a name,
no pleasure, but the compass of the body
stretching everywhere, the way a moth begins, squeezing out
of one life into another more swift and brief.

A Few Bright Leaves

Steve Dieffenbacher

Meditation along Bear Creek, near Talent

First she parted from light,
going gladly into grayness.
Then she receded from water
as pools with too much rain.
Then it was the air she left
for its edge of ice and snow.
All she carries are a few bright leaves
bumping along the stream,
oval and perfect
in the constancy of water.

Holding

Vincent Wixon

What you hold fits into the palm
like an egg in the nest—
so light you are taken aback
as when the jay lands on your finger
to take the crumb. How can
something so light be so blue
and its voice jerk you from sleep
when it torments the cat?

When the bats at the Shakespeare Festival
snare insects in their palms,
the actors carry on, of course,
as they are trained to do, but the audience
is drawn to the staggering flight
through the lights and cries out
while the bats, too, go about their business.

A baseball in the hand is perfect—
size, weight, stitches—and you know
to throw with speed and bite you must
hold it loosely, two fingers across the seams,
and balanced on the thumb and third finger.
As with many things, to hold fast
ruins the effect.

Where We Stand

Jonah Bornstein

Buckhorn Springs, Hwy 66

I want to take you with me,
erase the fractures and tend
again a garden planted with seeds
of unknown origin, to wait
for summer, when we unearth
the shy flames of discord.

I cannot shed the weapons
I have wrought, cannot clip
the limbs that balance
me—but I can be a brace
against the rapids that plunge
around you, I can be a bridge

for you to walk across; look down
into the river and you will see
the patterns of trees, the shadows
of leaves, the form of my love for you.

Do not fold yourself into the crib
of ice cast in the rocks
at the headwaters;
it holds nothing but sorrow—
a rote student of the past
frozen at the edge of our lives.

I want to rise from the base
of the gorge, extend up to you,
your reflection rippling
on the surface, because I love you
and I am drawing enough water
to hold us both a long time.

Northern Basin and Range

Desert Song

Jonah Bornstein

I

I will go to sacrifice myself
on the rock of my forefathers
for the silence of my thought and love
exhales dust of my weightless life.
If I could I would untie the towline,
drift off in my million particles, gathering
nothingness above the atmosphere.

Against the stone there will be a knife.
I require no altar, only flames to gather this flesh,
to send it up to reach my vision.

II

I have come to unburden myself.
I will sing this new idea.
The lizards will grow voices
and the desert will rise up in song.
I will not lift up my hand or thought
        against myself anymore.

III

I have turned from my sons
as if they were part of the unending landscape,
filaments of the desert that I order to lie down or rise up.
I will not do this anymore.

IV

I lie down in the sands of Mariah. The winds rise and work
the smooth dunes. In the desert night their voices
come from all sides; they rinse my body
with cool soughs and rough sands,
until only song lifts from my pores
and I walk from this place of sacrifice.

Rain Dance

Danae Yurgel

thirsty root of sage
beg down rain
from a deaf sky

the spring is drying

starving creek chants
over sharp stone
dusty wind drones in cottonwoods

Drought Dirge

Ellen Waterston

One mile up bone-dry road bawling
calves trip alongside mothers' gaunt half
notes. Droning phone lines in the heat
sag to breaking point from weight of sere
discords. The ransacked hide of a deer lies
scored, pitched, fly-less in the draw, clef
of sun-cured skin foretelling a waterless future.
The fretted ribs and fractured femur intone
crevasses, flats, clefts, sand bars, sharp
mountain peaks, ancient tremors. The same
in one—buck and hide of this land stretched
thin beyond recall. In the parched creek below
an antler pierces the stagnant muck, recording
the receding watermark. I part the scum with
my stick: a buck, its head still perfectly intact.
With my baton I poke the lip, the jowl. Loosed,
fur, fowl flesh floats gently off the face—pink,
bloodless. The jaw, now buoyant, opens—
a sluggish yawn or wide-mouthed scream.
One blind, pickled eye stares up at everything.

Harney Lake

Ellen Waterston

When the land said stop talking, I stopped
moving, as though words were needed to keep going,
to soften the blow of lava smashed across this scape,
to deflect the unrelenting gaze of land meeting sky halfway,
to guide my deaf hand across rockbound whispers,
to mourn the lupine's colorful daring, now squelched by the heat,
and warn the streams, giddy off the Steens,
that from this alkaline basin there is no escape.

Nowhere Called Home

Ellen Waterston

we drive the long way
past sagebrush and juniper
veer off Route Twenty

horses hightail it
prairie dogs fold tiny hands
cows raise up their heads

the valley narrows
we shadow the riverbed
to nowhere called home

Harney County Haiku

Ellen Waterston

Day floods the prairie
Lone rider goes at a lope
The fence line is down

Eastern Oregon

Vincent Wixon

The sun blazes here.
Huge cottonwoods force darkness
inside small frame houses where old women
whose men are dead and sons didn't come back
move in the dark touching pictures on parlor walls
while outside dust devils glide across the dragged grey fields.

Every Dust Mote

Ellen Waterston

I'm headed for Alice's. Been five years.
Couldn't get here till now. No good
reason I can recall. I see she's gone…
for good. Rye has run wild, badger
holes pock road of molten crush
that drifts easy along lush to hop-
scotch of house and out buildings.

The garden gate, mourning absent
push of her palm, warms to mine.
Lonely wind greens to gold, creek
spawns spring—lilac, gooseberry,
bumble and quail. Barrels pop
in the sun, hummingbird makes
a run, bees suckle Russian thistle,
corrugated metal stretches and snaps.
Every dust mote carries light
on its back. Every mote carries light.

Haven't seen you in a minute, she'd say
even if a year. Every moment bright.
Her eyes blue prisms startling fires.

Earl, he'd fly over weekly, look for
chimney smoke, code for Alice okay
or not. One hard winter, she laid herself
out flat in coveralls, cap. Semi-circled

her arms and legs in the snow. Later
Earl air-dropped hay for her cows.

Come spring, the sun melted her angel
print. The grass beneath sprouted wings.
Now I lie inside the fiery circle of her last
breath, feel the hill heave under me.
Her still life hovers over this high
desert push of land, prow of rock.

I'd been meaning to come.
She'd always said use just a little hurry
in life, in case you are right, in case
you are wrong. Every dust mote
carries light on its back. Every dust
mote carries light. Every mote carries light.

Epilogue

A Thousand Friends of Rain

Kim Stafford

I want to be rain scattering everywhere, licking
  down the long bamboo of a ryegrass stem to the
  dark Oregon earth.

I want to be rain's drum on barn roof and oak leaf,
  on juniper and windshield and salal.

I want to seethe wet into the pungent heart of sage.
  I want to trickle down the eagle's neck.
  I want to blur the ink on a document left outside.
  I want to educate with sensation.

I want to be a filament of Owyhee and Grand Ronde,
  Molalla, Nehalem, and Rogue. I want to throng
  the canyon they call Umpqua, and thunder
  Deschutes to Columbia.

But I want to be the unnamed rivulet, too,
  the silver thread a child finds with fingers
  and tongue. I want to start there, with the
  little ones, and school them to my cause.

I don't want to be a tyrant over my children,
  stealing their world before their hands are
  big enough to touch it gently, leaf by leaf.

I don't want to tarnish my father's gift,
my brother's heritage, this place where they
came home to die. This place must remain.

I want to learn from the sun to be generous, unafraid
as I spangle over the ghost town of Blitzen.
I want to learn to love every face and working
hand, to soothe the convict walking gray in
the prison yard, and the vagabond seeking not
a bridge to cross, but to sleep under. Strawberry
worker bent in the fields, how can I come gently
to touch your shoulder, *compadre* in our times?

I want to travel through trouble untroubled,
to plunge down the sewer drain, bubble in
the dark turmoil of grease and soot, the grief
and confusion of daily work, and then flow on,
spread out, rise up clear in mist and return
to my native ways.

They say Republican and Democrat. I say the
people of rain. They say cityfolk and
redneck (my neighbors Alonzo and Sunny).
I say hospitable tribe of the rain. I say rain
today in the gray of Portland and the dusty
green of high desert walking rain. They say for
and against. I say friend and friend, friend and
friend in midsummer Oregon rain.

I want to say we look back to Oregon before we
knew that name—back to cedar canoe,
to tribal legend and pioneer kerosene lamp,
we look back to know our story, to know our
opportunity: we can make an Oregon from
those same elements of woman and man,
of child and grandmother, of November night
by Siuslaw cedar, and midsummer dawn at
Rowena, of basalt and maple and rain. We can
make an Oregon that braids the old and the
not yet known. This is the whole work we do.

So be my dancing partner here. It's all one circle
by now from gentry to rude mechanical,
all one spinning world of rain. Vote rain.
Spend rain. Save and squander rain. Teach
your children rain. Oregon rain will be
our shrine, our grotto. I want to ask you into
the rain, the thousand little hands of rain.

At Kiger Gorge, I want to ask you to stand at
the rim and listen. At Oneonta, I want to
ask you to remember what you love.
At Perpetua, I want you to tell someone
what you love, but not with words, with what
you do. At Applegate, I want you to witness
for something bigger than the feast of all you
have felt and known. It is there, before you,

at any empty place, where water gleams
in the meadow, and last light touches the
mountain. At Fort Rock, and clear on down
to Hart Mountain I want to ask you to be
in the shine, the chill and dizzy spin of
midsummer Oregon rain today. Be friend.
We have everything to gain. Be native in
the way you take the wet wood hand of rain.

Contributors

Diane Averill is the author of two chapbooks and two full-length books of poetry, most recently *Beautiful Obstacles* by Blue Light Press. She was twice a finalist for the Oregon Book Award in Poetry. Her poems have been included in several anthologies such as *The Carnegie-Mellon Anthology of Poetry*, *From Here We Speak: An Anthology of Oregon Poetry*, and *Ravishing Disunities*, a book of ghazals by English speaking poets. She has been published in many literary magazines, including the *Bloomsbury Review*, *CALYX*, and *Poetry Northwest*. She won an award for the best poem by a graduate student while attending the University of Oregon and has received a grant from Literary Arts. She lives in Beavercreek.

David Axelrod is the author of three collections of poems. The most recent, *The Cartographer's Melancholy*, won the 2004 Spokane Poetry Prize. He is a previous recipient of the Kay Deeter Poetry Prize, the Carolyn Kizer Award, and artist and publisher fellowships from Literary Arts. Along with his wife and colleague, Jodi Varon, he edits the literary and fine arts journal *basalt*. His essays and poems appear in *Alaska Quarterly Review*, *Boulevard*, *Cimarron Review*, *Kenyon Review*, *Luna*, *Willow Springs*, and *Quarterly West*, among others. A professor of English at Eastern Oregon University, where he has taught for the past eighteen years, Axelrod recently returned from a year of teaching in Germany. He is currently at work on a new collection of poems, *Treason*, as well as Book Two of his epic poem, *The Kingdom at Hand*, and a novella, *What Vanished Remains as Something That Vanished*.

Judith Barrington was born in Britain and has lived for the past twenty-five years in Oregon. She is the author of three books of poetry: *Horses and the Human Soul* (Story Line Press, 2004), *Trying to be an Honest Woman* (The Eighth Mountain Press, 1985), and *History and Geography* (The Eighth Mountain Press, 1989). *Lifesaving: A Memoir* won the Lambda Book Award in 2001 and was a finalist for the PEN/Martha Albrand Award for the Art of the Memoir. Her awards include the The Dulwich Festival International Poetry Prize (U.K.), a Freedom of Expression Award from the ACLU, and Oregon Literary Arts' Steward H. Holbrook Award.

Jonah Bornstein's published books include *We Are Built of Light*, *A Path through Stone*, and *Voices from the Siskiyous*. His poem "Night Blooming Men" was nominated for a Pushcart Prize in 2000. His poems have appeared in *i.e.*, *one fare*, *violet*, *West Wind Review*, and the nationally acclaimed anthology *September 11, 2001, American Writers Respond* (Etruscan Press), edited by William Heyen. Bornstein was co-founder and director of the Ashland Writers Conference from 1997 to 2001. He has won various prizes including the Coulter Prize for poetry from the University of California, an Academy of American Poets Prize, the inaugural Southern Oregon Prize for service to the regional writing community, and an Oregon State Poetry Association Prize. He teaches poetry and literature at Southern Oregon University in Ashland where he lives with his wife, the painter Rebecca Gabriel. They have two grown sons.

Margaret Chula is a poet, teacher, performer, and founding editor of *Katsura Press*. Her five collections of poetry include *Grinding My Ink* and *Shadow Lines*, recipients of Haiku Society of America Book Awards; *This Moment*; *Always Filling, Always Full*; and her most recent collection, *The Smell of Rust*. Chula has collaborated with her husband, photographer John Hall, and musicians and dancers for performances in Portland, New York, Boston, Ottawa, Krakow, and Kyoto. These have been supported by grants from the Regional Arts and Culture Council and Oregon Literary Arts. From 1980 to 1992, she lived in Kyoto, Japan, where she taught creative writing at Doshisha Women's College and studied ikebana, woodblock printing, and zazen. She lives in Portland.

Steve Dieffenbacher has lived in southern Oregon since 1989, where he works as an editor and nature columnist for the *Medford Mail Tribune*. He has won numerous journalism awards for writing, photography, and design. His poetry has been published in many regional magazines including *Fireweed*, *Manzanita Quarterly*, *The Pointed Circle*, *Mountains and Rivers*, and *West Wind Review*. His poems are also included in the book-length cycle of poems, *A Path Through Stone* (1995) and in *Voices of the Siskiyous* (2006). His own chapbook, *At the Boundary*, was published in 2001. His poems are also included in the anthology, *Labyrinth: Poems and Prose* (2001) and in the collection, *Intri-*

cate Homeland: Collected Writings from the Klamath Siskiyou (2000). He is currently working on a book of poems about the Southwest desert. He lives in Talent near the eastern edge of the Siskiyous.

Barbara Drake's poetry chapbook, *Small Favors*, was recently published by Traprock Press. She is also the author of *Peace at Heart: An Oregon Country Life*, a collection of personal essays published by Oregon State University Press; *Writing Poetry*, a college-level creative writing textbook published by Heinle (formerly Harcourt); and several collections of poetry including *What We Say to Strangers* and *Love at the Egyptian Theatre*. Drake earned her BA and MFA degrees from the University of Oregon, subsequently lived in Michigan for sixteen years, and taught at Michigan State University before returning to Oregon in 1983. Since that time she has been teaching at Linfield College where she is a full professor. She and her husband live on a small farm in Yamhill County where they raise sheep, grow wine grapes, and enjoy entertaining their grandchildren.

Charles Goodrich is the author of a volume of poems, *Insects of South Corvallis*, and a collection of essays about nature, parenting, and building his own house, *The Practice of Home*. A professional gardener for twenty-five years, he presently works as program director for the Spring Creek Project for Ideas, Nature, and the Written Word at Oregon State University. He lives near the confluence of the Marys and Willamette Rivers in Corvallis.

Janice Gould is of mixed European and Konkow descent and grew up in Berkeley, California. She is a graduate of U.C. Berkeley, where she received degrees in linguistics and English, and of the University of New Mexico, where she earned a PhD in English. Her poetry has been published in many journals and anthologies, and she has won awards for her writing from the National Endowment for the Arts and the Astraea Foundation. Her books of poetry include *Beneath My Heart*, *Earthquake Weather*, and *Alphabet*. She is co-editor of *Speak to Me Words: Essays on American Indian Poetry* (University of Arizona). Gould recently completed a three-year term as the Hallie Ford Chair in creative writing at Willamette University.

Leanne Grabel teaches language arts to incarcerated teenage girls at Rosemont School in Portland. She is a poet, performer, and the mother of two teenage daughters. She has published poems and social commentary in a variety of literary magazines and publications, including *Salt*, *Fireweed*, *Stripped*, *Plazm*, *Clinton Street Quarterly*, *Portland Tribune*, *The Oregonian*, and *Bluestocking*. She is the author of numerous books of poetry, including *Short Poems by a Short Person* (Quiet Lion Press, 2002), *Anne Sexton Was a Sexpot* (Del Gado Press, 2003), and *Lonesome and Very Quarrelsome Heroes* (26 Books, 2003). Grabel's poetry-based theatrical shows "One Woman Shoe," "The Circus of Anguish and Mirth," "Anger: The Musical," and "The Lighter Side of Chronic Depression," have been performed on various Portland stages. Grabel graduated from Stanford University, has just finished an autobiographical novel entitled *The First Part*, and is currently beginning work on a full-length performance piece about methamphetamine and how it has impacted the children she teaches.

James Grabill's eighth book of poems, *An Indigo Scent after the Rain* (Lynx House Press, 2003), was selected as a finalist for the Oregon Book Award for Poetry. In 1995, his collection of poems *Poem Rising Out of the Earth and Standing Up in Someone* was awarded the Oregon Book Award for Poetry, and his gathering of essays and poems, *Through the Green Fire*, was chosen as a finalist for the Oregon Book Award for Creative Nonfiction. *October Wind* (Sage Hill Press, 2006) and *Finding the Top of the Sky* (Lost Horse Press, 2005), a collection of personal essays, are his latest books. His work has appeared widely in periodicals across the country such as *The Common Review*, *East West Journal*, *The New Age Journal*, *Poetry Northwest*, *Poetry East*, *Field*, *Willow Springs*, *Windfall*, and *kayak*. He lives in Portland.

George Hitchcock is the author of eleven collections of poetry, five produced plays, two novels, two story collections and many miscellaneous prose pieces. He received the C.E.S. Wood Award for Lifetime Achievement by the Oregon Book Awards, 2004. He lives in Eugene, Oregon, and was editor of the well-known poetry magazine, *kayak*, for twenty years, for which he received several national awards.

Barbara LaMorticella co-hosts *Talking Earth*, a poetry program on KBOO radio. In 1997, her second collection of poems, *Rain on Waterless Mountain*, was a finalist for the Oregon Book Award. In 2000 she was the recipient of the first Oregon Literary Fellowship for Women Writers, and, in 2005, she was awarded the Stewart H. Holbrook Award by Literary Arts. She has edited or co-edited three anthologies of Portland poetry. She has given over two hundred poetry readings, and her work has appeared in many anthologies, including *From Here We Speak*, the poetry volume of the Oregon Literature Series. She lives in the hills outside Portland.

Robert Hill Long was raised and educated in North Carolina. He has taught creative writing at the University of Oregon since 1991. His books include *The Power to Die*, *The Work of the Bow*, and *The Effigies*. He has received fellowships from the NEA (1988 and 2005) and the Oregon Arts Commission (1997). His work has been anthologized in *Best American Poetry*, *Flash Fiction*, and *Web del Sol*, and over the past thirty years has appeared in journals across the United States.

Richard Mack is the author of two books of poetry and essays, *Against a Western Sky* and *Reflections in a Western River*. One of his essays was a finalist for the *Oregon Quarterly* contest. His prose and poetry have been published in such journals as *Wind Literary Review*, *South Dakota Review*, *Clearwater Journal*, *Cape Rock*, *Branches*, *Green's Magazine*, *Denver Post*, *Circus Maximus*, and *Palouse Review*. Mack feels at home in the American West, having lived and worked in Oregon, Colorado, Washington, California, and Idaho. His career as a public school administrator and university professor took him to Micronesia, Guam, Japan, and throughout the deserts and mountains of eastern Oregon. He lives in LaGrande with his wife, Margo, and they own and operate Windwhistle Stables and Arena.

David Memmott has published four books of poetry and a story collection. His most recent book, *Watermarked* (Traprock Books, 2004), received four Pushcart Prize nominations. He is finishing work on a new collection, *In Shadow of Redtail: A Seasonal Round*. He has published in numerous magazines and anthologies, including *Interzone*, *Salt: An Oregon Coastal Poetry An-*

thology, and *Alchemy of Stars: An Anthology of Rhysling Award Winners.* One of his short stories won an award from Worldwide Writers, Inc., and his essay was recently posted on *Web del Sol*'s Writers at Work. Memmott is a Fishtrap Fellow and twice received publishing fellowships from Oregon Literary Arts, Inc. He is the editor and publisher of Wordcraft of Oregon, LLC, and serves on the Board of Directors of RondeHouse Media Arts Konsortium, a nonprofit group that sponsors a reading series in La Grande.

Amy Klauke Minato is the author of *The Wider Lens* (Ice River Press, 2004). Her poetry has been published in national and regional magazines and included in *From Here We Speak: An Anthology of Oregon Poetry.* She holds both an MFA in Creative Writing and an MS in Environmental Studies from the University of Oregon. Her poetry has been recognized with a 2003 Oregon Literary Arts Fellowship and her prose with a Walden Fellowship. She currently teaches reading and writing workshops in the Portland area, but she thinks of the Wallowa Mountains as her home.

Erik Muller is retired from a career of teaching college writing in Coos Bay and Eugene. He is the publisher of Traprock Books and one of the founding editors of *Fireweed: Poetry of Oregon.* He has written essays about Josephine Miles and Vern Rutsala for the Western Writers Series from Boise State University. He lives in Eugene.

Paulann Petersen is a former Stegner Fellow at Stanford University whose poems have appeared in many publications including *Poetry,* the *New Republic, Prairie Schooner,* and *Wilderness Magazine.* She has three chapbooks—*Under the Sign of a Neon Wolf, The Animal Bride,* and *Fabrication.* She has published three full-length collection of poems: *The Wild Awake* (Confluence Press, 2002), *Blood-Silk* (Quiet Lion Press, 2004), and *A Bride of Narrow Escape* (Cloudbank Books, 2006). Her work has been selected for *Poetry Daily* on the Internet, and for Poetry in Motion, which puts poems on busses and light rail cars in the Portland metropolitan area. The winner of two Carolyn Kizer Awards, she has been on the faculty for the Creative Arts Community at Menucha and has given workshops for Oregon Writers Workshop, Oregon State Poetry Association, and Mountain Writers Series. She serves on the board for Friends of William Stafford, organizing the annual William Stafford Birthday Events.

Vern Rutsala's *The Moment's Equation* was a finalist for the National Book Award in 2005. His other recent books include *A Handbook for Writers: New and Selected Prose Poems* and *How We Spent Our Time*. The latter received the Akron Poetry Prize. He has received a Guggenheim Fellowship, two NEA grants, a Masters Fellowship from the Oregon Arts Commission, Juniper Prize, two Carolyn Kizer Poetry Prizes, and the Kenneth O. Hanson Award.

Ralph Salisbury, professor emeritus at the University of Oregon, is the author of two books of short fiction and eight books of poetry, the most recent of which is *War in the Genes* (Cherry Grove Collections, 2006). *Rainbows of Stone* (University of Arizona Press, 2000) was chosen by Maxine Kumin as a finalist in the Oregon Book Awards. He has received many awards, among them a Rockefeller Foundation Creative Writing Residency at the Villa Serbelloni in Bellagio, Italy; the Chapelbrook Award; the Northwest Poetry Award; three Fulbright professorships, to Germany and Norway; and an Amparts (USIS) lectureship in India. For six years the editor-in-chief of *Northwest Review*, Salisbury also has edited *A Nation Within*, an anthology of contemporary Native American writing, and has co-translated two books by Sami (Lapplander) poet Nils-Aslak Valkeappaa.

Peter Sears has published poems in *The Atlantic, The Christian Science Monitor, Field, Mother Jones, The New York Times, Orion, Rolling Stone,* and *The Saturday Review*. His book, *The Brink,* won the 1999 Peregrine Smith Poetry Competition (Gibbs Smith Publisher, 2000) and the Western States Book Award in Poetry. With Kim Stafford, Sears co-founded Friends of William Stafford in 1997. He lives in Corvallis.

Floyd Skloot is the author of five collections of poetry, most recently *The End of Dreams* (LSU Press, 2006) and *Approximately Paradise* (Tupelo Press, 2005). He won the 2001 Oregon Book Award in Poetry for *The Evening Light* (Story Line Press, 2001), and his poetry has been included in *The Best Spiritual Writ-*

ing 2001, *The Penguin Book of the Sonnet*, and such magazines as *The Atlantic*, *Harper's*, *Poetry*, *American Scholar*, *Sewanee Review*, *Hudson Review*, *Southern Review*, and *Boulevard*. He has won two Pushcart Prizes. An essayist and novelist, Skloot recently won the 2004 PEN Center USA Literary Award in Creative Nonfiction and the 2003 Oregon Book Award in Creative Nonfiction. He lives in Portland.

Kim Stafford is the founding director of the Northwest Writing Institute and author of *The Muses Among Us: Eloquent Listening and Other Pleasures of the Writer's Craft* and *A Thousand Friends of Rain: New & Selected Poems*, as well as a dozen other books of poetry and prose. He sees language as the fundamental human alternative to violence and urges everyone to write.

William Stafford authored sixty books of poetry and prose, including *Traveling through the Dark*, which won the National Book Award. He was a faculty member at Lewis and Clark College for thirty years, and he also traveled widely as a witness for literature and peace. Mr. Stafford was poetry consultant to the Library of Congress, the position now known as Poet Laureate.

Mark Thalman's poetry has been widely published in small presses, college reviews, anthologies, and e-zines for the last three decades. His work has appeared in *Carolina Quarterly*, *Chariton Review*, *CutBank*, *Natural Bridge*, *Pennsylvania Review*, *Sou'wester*, *Texas Review*, *Wisconsin Review*, and *Whetstone* among others. Thalman's work appeared recently in *Many Mountains Moving*. One of his poems was a top finalist for their 2006 *MMM* Poetry Online and In Print Contest. He also won second place in the 2006 Marylhurst Review poetry contest and an honorable mention. He received his MFA from the University of Oregon, and he teaches English in the public schools. Thalman lives in Forest Grove with his wife, Carole, and their two golden retrievers, Sherlock Holmes and Agatha Christie.

George Venn has written and published four books, most recently *West of Paradise* (1999), a finalist for the Oregon Book Award in poetry. In 2005, his multi-genre collection *Marking the Magic Circle* (1987) was selected by the Oregon Cultural Heritage Commission as one of the best Oregon books in the past two hundred years. He has edited sixteen works, including the 2,000 page, six-volume *Oregon Literature Series* (1993-94) for which he, as General Editor, received the Stewart Holbrook Award. His poems have been widely published in periodicals and anthologized in seventeen different state, regional, and national collections, most recently in *Teaching with Fire: Poetry that Sustains the Courage to Teach* (2003). As a poet, he was awarded a Pushcart Prize and the Andres Berger Prize from Northwest Writers, Inc. His prose has been published in over thirty different periodicals and anthologized in sixteen collections, most recently in *World Views and the American West* (2000). A professor of English and Writer-in-Residence emeritus at Eastern Oregon University, he's given more than two hundred off-campus readings and workshops, including an appointment as Writer-on-Tour for Western States Arts Foundation. His forthcoming works include the monograph *Soldier to Advocate: C.E.S. Wood's 1877 Legacy* (Wordcraft of Oregon, 2006) and essays in *RondeDance* and *Idaho Yesterdays*.

Ellen Waterston's collection of poetry, *I Am Madagascar* (Ice River Press, 2004), won the 2005 WILLA Award in Poetry. Her award-winning memoir, *Then There Was No Mountain: The Parallel Odyssey of a Mother and Daughter Through Addiction*, was selected by the *Oregonian* as one of the top ten books of the year, earned her an appearance on *Good Morning America*, and was a WILLA finalist. Her poetry has appeared in publications including *Oregon East*, *Cascades East*, *High Desert Journal*, *Honoring Our Rivers*, *Clearwater Journal*, *West Wind Review*, *Windfall*, *A Trek Through Eastern Oregon By Poet*, *RANGE*, *Anthology of American Poets*, *Living Spiritually In A Consumer Society* and in the Houghton Mifflin anthologies *Woven In The Wind* and *Crazy Woman Creek*. In December 2003, Waterston received the Special Literary Fellowship for Women Writers given by Oregon's Literary Arts, Inc. She was awarded a 2004 Ucross Foundation residency and the two-month Fishtrap Writer-in-Residence in 2005. She is working on a novel and a second collection of poetry.

Ingrid Wendt's five books of poems include *Surgeonfish* (winner of the 2004 Editions Prize), *The Angle of Sharpest Ascending* (winner of the 2003 Yellowglen Award), and *Singing the Mozart Requiem* (winner of the Oregon Book

Award). She co-edited the anthologies *In Her Own Image: Women Working in the Arts* and *From Here We Speak: An Anthology of Oregon Poetry*. Her teaching guide, *Starting With Little Things: A Guide to Poetry Writing in the Classroom*, is in its sixth printing. Her work has appeared in *No More Masks! An Anthology of Twentieth-Century American Women Poets* and in numerous literary journals and anthologies. Winner of the Carolyn Kizer Award and the D.H. Lawrence Fellowship, Wendt has been a three-time Fulbright professor to Germany and guest lecturer at several international universities. Born in Aurora, Illinois, she has lived in Oregon since 1971.

Rob Whitbeck is a farmer and laborer living in Wheeler County in eastern Oregon. He is the author of two full-length collections of poetry, *Oregon Sojourn* and *The Taproot Confessions* (Pygmy Forest Press, 2001 and 2003). In 2004, a CD of Whitbeck's poems drawn from both volumes was released under the title *Western Cross*. In 2005 he was awarded a fellowship from Literary Arts and won The Working Peoples' Poetry Competition, sponsored by Partisan Press. Currently he is at work on a book-length narrative called *Slaid's Fire*.

Patricia Wixon's poetry has appeared in *Oregon English, Oregon Centennial, HUBBUB*, and several other literary magazines. She has been a guest columnist for *Fireweed*, and has had essays published in professional journals and anthologies. She is on the board of directors of Friends of William Stafford and has been a researcher for the William Stafford Archives for twelve years, most recently producing the CD, *The Unknown Good In Our Enemies: William Stafford Reads Poems Of Reconciliation*. Wixon lives in Ashland.

Vincent Wixon is the author of two books of poetry, *The Square Grove* (Traprock Books, 2006) and *Seed* (May Day Press, 1993). His poems appear in two anthologies, *From Here We Speak: An Anthology of Oregon Poetry* and *Weathered Pages*. He and Michael Markee produced two videos with William Stafford, *What the River Says* and *The Life of the Poem*, and one with Lawson Inada, *What It Means To Be Free*. With Paul Merchant, director of the William Stafford Archive, Wixon has edited two books on writing by William Stafford, *Crossing Unmarked Snow* and *The Answers Are Inside the Mountains* (University of Michigan Press). He and his wife, Patricia, live in Ashland and are long-time poetry editors for *Jefferson Monthly*, the public radio program guide for southern Oregon and northern California.

Danae Yurgel lives on the breaks between the Minam-Wallowa and Grande Ronde Rivers in the north end of Union County. She works as a program co-ordinator for library outreach to homebound seniors and in her spare time runs a martial arts dojo with her partner of fifteen years, grows a small farm business selling herbs and flowers, and occasionally is employed as a trainer and skills facilitator. In addition, she is a freelance artist, mask-maker, writer, and is working towards her college degree. Her poems have been published locally in *Oregon East, Clearwater Review*, the anthology *Third Season / Seven Poets*, and several small press poetry magazines. Her theater pieces were performed in the EOU New Play Series in 2003 and 2005. She has also par-ticipated in regional poetry readings and events.

Copyright Acknowledgments

Index of Titles and Authors

EDITING

KATRINA HILL

LAURA MEEHAN

EMILEE NEWMAN BOWLES

KRISTIN THIEL

CELESTE THOMPSON

LEAD: MATT WALKER

DESIGN

DAVID BANIS

KAREN BRATTAIN

WAYNE COFFEY

ABBEY GATERUD

ANGELA HODGE

JOANNA SCHMIDT

LEAD: MATT WALKER

MARKETING

TERRA CHAPEK

CANDY DAWSON

ELIZABETH FULLER

MCKENZIE GABY

LEAD: MONICA GARCIA

LAURA HOWE

OOLIGAN PRESS takes its name from a Native American word for the common smelt or candlefish, a source of wealth for millennia on the Northwest Coast and origin of the word "Oregon." Ooligan is a general trade press rooted in the rich literary life of Portland and the Department of English at Portland State University. In addition to publishing books that honor cultural and natural diversity, Ooligan is staffed by students pursuing masters degrees in an apprenticeship program under the guidance of a core faculty of publishing professionals. By publishing real books in real markets, students combine theory with practice; the press and the classroom become one.

Special thanks to Wayne Coffey and David Banis in the Portland State University Center for Spatial Analysis and Research for their patience, enthusiasm, and expertise.

Ooligan Press
PO Box 751
Portland OR 97207
www.publishing.pdx.edu
ooligan@pdx.edu

208